SELF-SABOTAGE:
THE ART OF SCREWING UP

Understanding the How, Where, When, and WHY We All Do It!

ROSA LIVINGSTONE, CHT.

BALBOA PRESS
A DIVISION OF HAY HOUSE

Copyright © 2016 Rosa Livingstone.

All rights reserved. No part of this book may be used or reproduced by any means, graphic, electronic, or mechanical, including photocopying, recording, taping or by any information storage retrieval system without the written permission of the author except in the case of brief quotations embodied in critical articles and reviews.

Balboa Press books may be ordered through booksellers or by contacting:

Balboa Press
A Division of Hay House
1663 Liberty Drive
Bloomington, IN 47403
www.balboapress.com
1 (877) 407-4847

Because of the dynamic nature of the Internet, any web addresses or links contained in this book may have changed since publication and may no longer be valid. The views expressed in this work are solely those of the author and do not necessarily reflect the views of the publisher, and the publisher hereby disclaims any responsibility for them.

The author of this book does not dispense medical advice or prescribe the use of any technique as a form of treatment for physical, emotional, or medical problems without the advice of a physician, either directly or indirectly. The intent of the author is only to offer information of a general nature to help you in your quest for emotional and spiritual well-being. In the event you use any of the information in this book for yourself, which is your constitutional right, the author and the publisher assume no responsibility for your actions.

Any people depicted in stock imagery provided by Thinkstock are models, and such images are being used for illustrative purposes only.
Certain stock imagery © Thinkstock.

Print information available on the last page.

ISBN: 978-1-5043-6122-4 (sc)
ISBN: 978-1-5043-6123-1 (hc)
ISBN: 978-1-5043-6124-8 (e)

Library of Congress Control Number: 2016910889

Balboa Press rev. date: 06/30/2016

ABOUT THE AUTHOR

I stilled my inner critic and went out on a limb.

Having finally graduated and certified as a Clinical Hypnotherapist, I knew one thing for certain, I'd found my passion. And boy, had I searched. It took a very traumatic event in my life to help me truly evaluate who I was, what my strengths were, and what I needed to change within myself to become who I had always felt I could be.

I'd love to say that the event was a hypnotherapy session of my own. I only wish that were true. In 2005, my four year old son, Jordan, developed an unexpected illness. Suddenly learning that he had a brain tumor, and that it was at a critical stage, I was thrown into an abyss. My world froze, and I coped by staying focused in the moment. My career was put on hold. My dreams were shelved. The most important thing to me was helping Jordan get through the surgeries, the loss of mobility, and the fear and confusion, as well as guiding his older brother, Andrew, to adjust to all this chaos and assuring him that what he felt was just as important.

I took a leave of absence from my management position in the hotel industry, understanding that the scope of my work demands wouldn't allow me the flexibility to care for Jordan.

I examined my strengths and weaknesses with a fine-tooth comb, recognizing that for many years I'd wanted to do work that gave back and that helped others. Serendipity stepped in and I found hypnotherapy. I can't tell you what intrigued me more, the therapy part or the hypnosis part, but I ran with it - and the rest is history.

It's been a wonderful journey of self-growth. I did my own inner work in class and still continue to do so. We are all 'works in progress', and healing doesn't happen overnight.

Over many years of dedicated study and practice, I have learned that healing is natural. It happens when we want it to and when we are willing to dig deep to get it. We don't have to manufacture change. All the tools we need are inside us. We just need the right key to open the tool box. Because I chose to change an inner belief that had me feeling unworthy, I was able to create a really good life with a wonderful husband who encourages me and is my biggest cheerleader, and I have a deeper and more loving relationship with my two sons, Andrew and Jordan, who are the joy in my heart and my best achievements so far!

I have the greatest respect for my clients for having the courage to face their fears and self-sabotaging ways without having had previous experience dealing with the subconscious mind. It takes guts to be willing to step outside the walls we erect around ourselves. Our only limitations are those we set for ourselves, and those limitations were erected at a time when we didn't have the choices, abilities, experience, or control that we have as adults.

By working diligently on ourselves, we experience what I call 'the shift'. When we have paradigm shifts, it's how we feel that indicates the shift. It shows up when we notice that we feel better, think more clearly, and react more positively in a situation, or to a challenge. This is when we shift from the old behavior patterns (which come from old thoughts, feelings, and beliefs) to new patterns of thoughts, feelings, and behaviors that are healthier for us.

If you have any questions or comments, I welcome them. You can reach me at www.aloadoffyourmind.com

Welcome to the journey.

DEDICATION

I am deeply grateful to all those that encouraged me, supported me and believed in my ability to write this book, offering guidance and sometimes, a 'good talking to' when I tried to sabotage myself. Without them, I wouldn't have gone the distance.

I am tremendously thankful to my amazing Husband, John, who has always been "The President" of my Fan Club and who encouraged me to write this book for many years. Thank you for making me laugh and smile throughout this process. All the hugs helped, too!

To my Sons, Andrew and Jordan, for teaching me to walk-the-walk, and for inspiring me to the best I can be.

To my Sister, Manuela, gratefulness for our shared upbringing and for always holding me up when I needed it.

To my Niece, Susana, who has inspired me to be courageous and to go out on a limb.

To my Parents, Gloria and Tony, for doing the best they could with what they knew at that time.

To Debbie, Natalie, and Mandy, for your loving friendship, for the time spent reading my draft and for cheering me on! And to Stacy, Delane, Tracey, Kim and Yane, for just being the best friends a girl could have.

To all of my clients, deep gratitude for allowing me to be part of their journey to healing so that I, too, could grow, heal and learn.

And I'm grateful for all my life experiences which hold within them the lessons I needed that allowed me to be here now. I could not have gotten to where I am without them.

CONTENTS

About the Author v
Dedication ix
Introduction xiii

Chapter 1 :   Self-sabotage - what is it, and why would
              anyone want to do that? 1
Chapter 2 :   Self-limiting behavior begins in childhood -
              the pivotal influences behind self-doubt 7
Chapter 3 :   Mind Works 101 15
Chapter 4 :   Blueprint of expectations 25
Chapter 5 :   How emotions drive our thoughts and actions .. 31
Chapter 6 :   Suppression, expression, and release 41
Chapter 7 :   Participant, observer, creator 50
Chapter 8 :   Critical self-talk - that nasty, 'dissing' voice in
              your head 60
Chapter 9 :   Negative influences that cause us to self-
              sabotage 67
Chapter 10 : Some areas in life where we let our saboteur
              get in the way 74
Chapter 11 : Self-sabotage and depression 77
Chapter 12 : Self-sabotage and anxiety 84
Chapter 13 : Self-sabotage, romance, and intimacy 90
Chapter 14 : Self-sabotage and weight 101

Chapter 15 : Self-sabotage and money 111
Chapter 16 : Letting your 'Greater than you think you are'
              plan guide you 118
Chapter 17 : A leap of faith with courage and strength 122
Chapter 18 : Defining your moment 127
Chapter 19 : Give up your story 132
Chapter 20 : Open up to trust! 137
Chapter 21 : Questions to ask yourself about all the
              good stuff that exists inside you 142
Chapter 22 : Commitment 149
Chapter 23 : Personal writings I'd like to share 154

"In order to understand, I destroyed myself."
*~**Fernando Pessoa***

INTRODUCTION

We all screw up! Each of us has an 'inner critic', judging our every action and instructing us on how to live our lives. It lives in the shadows, below the level of our conscious awareness. How much are we letting this big-mouthed mysterious inner critic mess with us? Are our actions based on our truest feelings and beliefs about ourselves, or are we living our lives based on our negative programming? These are questions I invite you to think about honestly, without fear or denial. Then observe the answers as they come to you, for they will come, if you listen.

I've thought about writing this book since 2008. The key word is 'thought'. It began with offering free information evenings to anyone who was willing to come and hear about how we all self-sabotage, what it is and why we do it. I've spoken publicly in my career on many occasions, but never about a subject that I believe in as much as I do this one - but it doesn't offer me a curtain to hide behind. I began to get excited about putting on paper what I had been explaining to groups of people in order to reach a larger audience. Educating and coaching are my passions!

I began working on chapter titles, playing with content, looking at book cover ideas and even attended an evening writing workshop. It all sounded so good, even if I'd never written anything other than private journals lamenting love and life, and dark poetry, also lamenting love and life. I had thought, 'This is the time!' with a fist pump in the air. But something began to happen to all this dizzying insight and euphoria. I'd been in the runner's stance, like the little girl I used to be, getting ready to run the 100 meter dash.

Then I started to hear a voice that just paralyzed me, saying 'You're going to bomb. No one's going to read your book. You're not good enough!' This last degrading comment was said so loudly I was sure others heard it outside my head. My inner critic decided this was the time to browbeat me and remind me of all the other ideas I've had that never went past the starting line and fizzled before the bang of the starter gun. Regardless of what my head was saying, my runner's lunge 'ready' position was awesome, if I do say so myself. That negative, authoritative voice that sounded much like my mother's had me cowering on the floor in full fetal position, my hand over my eyes and my thumb in my mouth like the skinny kid I used to be, feeling too weak to stand up for myself.

I saw, for the first time and with startling clarity, that I was self-sabotaging! Me, the person who thought she understood this concept from a professional standpoint but who hadn't looked at it on a personal level. Everyone, without exception, has a destructive inner voice that, given rein to do so, will sabotage our goals. This inner critic judges our every action and tells us, using a stern authoritative voice or a cajoling whine, how to live our lives. That voice actually has the ability to encourage us to act in ways that are self-destructive and to take actions that undermine us and hold us back from taking positive, healthy risks. Learning to deal effectively with our critical inner voice is central to all areas of life: personal development and self-esteem building, healthy relationships, and career success.

So the goal of this book is two-fold. It is for me, selfishly, to work through my own myopic point of view when it comes to what I can create for myself, what I can bring to the table, and most importantly, how I see myself and not worrying about how others see me. This creation is to help set me free! It's to help me get over my own fear of judgment, and to stop perpetuating all those things into my world that disempower me because I've let them do so. My goal is to embrace the saying, 'what other people think of me is none of my business'!

Secondly, it's meant to land in the hands of those who recognize that they, too, get in their own way. That they, too, have an inner critic that has to be toned down or silenced completely by being put on a new, healthy mind diet.

Within these pages I will do my best to enlighten you about what self-sabotage is, how we do it to ourselves, where it appears in our lives, when we do it, and most importantly, why we do it in the first place. At the end of this process, it will be up to you to choose to move towards living the life you want, using all that is inherently amazing within you, versus letting the life you're living now control you and prevent you from spreading your wings. It's time to fall madly and deeply in love with yourself, for only then will you see how amazing you are…and you are amazing!

Although I am a Clinical Hypnotherapist, this book is neither about hypnosis nor how to use hypnosis for self-change, although I encourage you to explore the idea. As a Mind Coach, I hope to feed your unlimited mind with information gathered from personal experience, client experiences, and general sources that will not only appeal to your logic but send a message to your inner critic that you're onto it and that you've got its number, because it will be listening as you take in the words, concepts, and ideas in this book. I will also suggest some ideas on how to address the self-sabotaging habits you face. There is room at the end of many of the chapters to write your thoughts about probing concepts and questions.

Change doesn't just miraculously happen. 'A miracle is just a shift in perception.' ~*A Course in Miracles*. Change is a life-long journey that, over time, yields amazing personal results, and it's for you to decide whether you are ready and willing to drop that gun you're using to shoot yourself in the foot, or if you want to go on being the foot that's kicking you in the ass.

> "Experience is not what happens to you. It's what you do with what happens to you."
> **~Aldous Huxley**

> "Life shrinks or expands in proportion to one's courage"
> **~Anais Nin**

If you reach for courage, which we all inherently have, you will have the ability to create what you dream of, and the world will become your classroom. If you choose to listen to the self-saboteur inside you, and hold onto fear, or allow it to ensnare you, then you are only a participant in your life, continuing to screw up, and living in your own self-imposed prison.

Take the leap!

*"I do nothing upon myself and
yet I am my own executioner"*

~John Donne

CHAPTER 1

Self-sabotage - what is it, and why would anyone want to do that?

The dictionary definition of sabotage is 'an act or process tending to hamper or hurt', or 'deliberate subversion', as well as 'any undermining of a cause or priority'. So the definition of self-sabotage would be 'any undermining of your own cause or priority, which hampers or hurts you'. Okay, then. Why would we want to sabotage ourselves? Why would we ever hurt ourselves? The answer is complicated, but an easy one, too. We make that choice.

We are self-sabotaging if:

- we settle for less than we really want;
- we often make the thought greater than the task;
- we find road-blocks on the way to our dreams;
- we are obsessive perfectionists;
- we second-guess our decisions or find it hard to simply make a decision;

- we always put others' needs before ours;
- we sell ourselves short;
- we constantly engage in negative self-talk.

Self-sabotage is all about programming. It's about the negative self-talk that takes place subconsciously, when we are not consciously aware of what that nasty voice is saying in the background of our minds. We're not consciously aware because we're not listening to it or for it. We can't take action against something we're not aware of.

Self-sabotage happens when the fear of making a mistake, screwing up, or getting something wrong overtakes our ability to take assertive, inspired action. When we're afraid and aren't sure what to do, we often end up doing nothing at all. We become overwhelmed, and a downward spiral overtakes us; sleepless nights, anxiety attacks, depression, and unending stress become our reality.

The doomsayer program of the mind protects beliefs that may be contrary to what we want. That function of belief protection is the stronghold of the subconscious mind, the single most powerful, goal-oriented mechanism known to man. I just can't say that enough!

The subconscious mind is programmed to find goals that fit belief systems that we formed early in life, and it's ruthlessly efficient. When faced with a goal that doesn't fit the belief, it finds the process like a worker ant. Let's say we have homework for a night course we're taking that will help get a promotion at work. And we find a zillion excuses not to do it. Excuses like 'I'm tired from working all day and need a break right now', or 'I have to do the laundry first or I won't have any clean clothes to wear to work tomorrow', or 'Maybe this isn't for me', or even 'I'll do it later when I have more energy (or time...or brain cells)'. Do any of these sound familiar? Are any of these excuses going to get us the promotion? It's true, dressing in clean, pressed clothes might make an impression on our boss, who is holding the keys to our future. It's also true, being bleary-eyed-tired might put a damper on that impression. Despite that, we know we need to finish the course so that we not only look good, but feel our confidence boosted, which will hike up our chances of getting that promotion that will increase our income and self-esteem.

Logically, we may know we have the drive and passion to climb the corporate ladder. After all, that's what encouraged us to throw our name in the hat in the first place, but we're self-aware enough to also recognize that we need the knowledge from this course for the new position.

So how is it that we can know that this course is vital to our professional growth, yet all that excitement and drive can deflate and shrivel like a three-day-old helium balloon?

It's because the subconscious mind has other plans for us, and those plans are based on a belief that we have about ourselves. That's scary, no? Because it's a subconscious belief, we aren't consciously aware of the belief and, at this point, we don't even remember what the belief is. Even scarier, isn't it?

Why doesn't willpower help us when we really think we want something? The problem is that willpower is a function of the conscious mind. Willpower is the energy behind an action, and we use it to move towards something, but it doesn't come from the powerful, goal-oriented subconscious mind, which means that willpower fizzles out in the face of the ruthless subconscious mind programming, which is like a pit bull on steroids.

Let's say that the deep-rooted belief in this instance is that we're not good enough. The subconscious mind will protect this belief because it's ours. We came to believe we weren't good enough at a time when we had no control of what was happening around us (Chapter 2 will clarify this point). This subconscious belief now extends to our professional life, so the subconscious mind sees our going for that promotion as a threat to its belief. The subconscious believes that in pursuit of our goal, we will ultimately be emotionally hurt because we're not good enough to handle the new responsibilities. It may also be acting on the perception that we might fail and feel devastated. We subconsciously buy into that.

So the inner mind begins the process of sabotaging us to ensure that we don't go through with pursuing that promotion. Our national defense department could really learn from this part of the mind. As our minds are imaginative, they can cook up countless ways of sabotaging our plans. The basis of all programming is the issue of self-belief and worthiness. There isn't an issue I've dealt with in my practice that, at its root, isn't based in the feeling of not being good enough. The programming uses our own feelings and thoughts to sabotage movement toward a goal that the subconscious sees as not being achievable. The subconscious isn't a realistic mind, or a judging mind. It's not doing all this to make us feel bad. In fact, it doesn't think at all! It's doing everything it knows to protect us, without judgment - and I'll get into that shortly.

Thus, slowly but surely (or quickly and surely), we begin to feel nervous, and doubt ourselves. We may or may not wonder where the excitement and drive went. Well, it was booted out the door along with our course texts. We find ways to avoid the task, and the thought of the task becomes greater than the task itself.

Let's look at how this all began, all the way back to the innocent children we were.

Notes:

"We cannot maintain joy in a state where we allow someone else to live our life for us. Most people do this because they feel that it is their responsibility to live to please others. This is not true. First and foremost, we must live impeccably and honestly to please ourself, in a kind and caring way."
~***Secrets of the Golden Spiral***

CHAPTER 2

Self-limiting behavior begins in childhood - the pivotal influences behind self-doubt

We all began our lives in a home with caregivers who either loved us or were indifferent in their care for us. We all have a story with a beginning. Regardless of our individual circumstances, we were all born into families made up of different structures, some with two parents and some with only one, but what is the same in every family is that all members individually carry their own inner programming, learned from their upbringing in the family unit, as well as the rules of right and wrong passed down from generation to generation.

Parental figures carry a major responsibility that they may not fully understand. Unlike a new DVD player, an infant doesn't come with a guidebook. There is no return policy how-to book or warranty attached to a newborn's foot at birth. As parents, we raise our fists to the heavens because of that lack of guidance when our children have tantrums at the mall or when they stretch our patience as teenagers. We use the only guidance and experience we can draw on: that which we learned as children from our own parents. How many times did you hear your mom or dad say 'In my day, kids were seen and not heard'? Or did you hear 'when I was a kid, if I talked back to my parents there'd be serious consequences'?

As children, our role was to learn and be guided. Our family's role was to teach and guide. It sounds simple, yet it's so far from that. Children don't have the opportunity to choose their beliefs, morals, and values. They follow those passed along by their family and any influential authorities, such as teachers, extended family, and religious figures. That's how they learn about their world and their place within it. We believed everything adults told us, unequivocally, because we assumed they knew everythin.

Studies show that our learning begins as early as the womb; that a fetus is already learning and has emotions. As Dr. Bruce Lipton illustrates in *The Biology of Belief*, the fetus has a connection to its own environment, as well as to events which happen outside its mother. These connections influence the physical and emotional development of the fetus. A fetus can sense its mother's emotions and other physical stimuli. It can hear what is happening outside its cocoon, and pick up on the tone of conversations within its hearing. In my practice, many of my clients have regressed to being in the womb, for it was there that they first experienced the emotional trauma that caused the emotional distress they were experiencing.

A woman who came to me to work through her inability to find a loving relationship regressed to a time in her mother's womb when she heard her mother say that she didn't want to be pregnant. Of course, she didn't consciously know what this actually meant at the time. She internalized her mother's sadness and this was imprinted. By following her feelings of sadness at the thought of being unlovable, we regressed to that initial sensitizing event in the womb. She was then able to interpret how she felt with words. That experience in the womb had begun a lifelong belief that she was unlovable and unwanted.

Children, even at the fetal stage, are aware of the world by how it feels. Because they have limited experience, they believe that they are the center of their world and their world consists of what's inside their bubble. Children will often feel that they are the cause of any problem or friction in their family, believing that it's their fault that someone else isn't happy. If only they'd been nicer, put away their toys, or listened, then mom or dad wouldn't fight, or be sad, or yell at each other.

In Freudian psychology, Dr. Freud described how children learn by using the pleasure principle, which is the instinctual seeking of physical and emotional pleasure and the avoidance of pain in order to satisfy physical and psychological needs. He stated that the mind avoids pain by seeking pleasure. Imagine a child getting into trouble just so that they can get attention. They don't understand restraint and they look for instant gratification. It brings to mind memories of my sons when they were small. When they wanted their diapers changed, they wailed to high-heaven until I attended to their needs, helping them feel better and gratifying their physical pleasure. When they wanted a cuddle and I was too busy, they cried loudly until I hurried to hug them, which gratified their emotional pleasure.

All children learn to be pleasers because they discover that when they are 'good', their parents will respond favorably. The child feels pleasure, assurance, and love when they please those who are most important to them. They try to please mom, dad, and their teachers in order to feel wanted, loved, and accepted. They learn very early on that certain behaviors are rewarded and they are called 'good', and so they feel good. Other behaviors are punished and they are called 'bad', so they feel bad. In their very simple way of thinking, pleasing equates to acceptance, and as adults, we continue to believe it.

Over time, trying to please others and yet not getting their emotional and physical needs met, children begin to fear that they are not good enough. They think they have fallen short of other peoples' expectations, and that leads to the fear of rejection, abandonment, and ultimately, being unloved. That fear leads to a journey of eroding self-esteem.

So how does this happen? We, as adults, logically rationalize that we are worthy of the things we desire, such as love, wealth, success, happiness, and health. However, as children, we don't have the ability to analyze our actions and those of others in a rational way.

For example, I had a client who re-experienced a four-year-old event when he accidentally broke his mom's vase that had belonged to his grandmother. His mom yelled at him and called him a 'bad boy'. He didn't break the vase on purpose.

Or another actual client experience, when the client, as a five-year-old girl, was having trouble learning her ABCs and her dad called her 'stupid'.

Both these childhood events left the children feeling unworthy and not good enough. They got it not only from the words of their parents, but from their tone of voice and body language. So, I ask you, was the little girl, or the little boy, stupid? Of course they weren't, but they thought so and didn't know that it wasn't true. The little girl only knew that if her father said she was stupid, she must be, even if she felt instinctually that she wasn't.

Often the first emotion felt during events like these is confusion. Children don't naturally feel bad, but if their mother or father says, directly or indirectly, that they are, then children believe it. Parents are our role-models, and so cannot be wrong. Life, logic and distance will prove that our parents are also human and make mistakes, but to a child, this is beyond their understanding, and the memory is permanently held in the subconscious even when the event is forgotten.

Do you recall at time in your past when you were made to feel small, inadequate, or helpless? This threatened your feelings of worthiness, and you've carried these feelings into your adulthood. Even if there are no examples you can come up with at this moment, it doesn't mean they don't exist. It's perceptual, and you have forgotten consciously what is remembered subconsciously.

It has been proven that if you encourage a child to believe that it is intelligent from a young age with kind words, gentle voice intonation, and loving gestures, the child will believe it and gain self-esteem and confidence. If you express to a child that it is bad from a young age in words, voice intonation, and gestures that are unloving, the child will believe it and will display fear, anxiety, and shyness in later life. We all become what we are told we are, and base our beliefs about our place and value in the world on non-verbal cues from role-models. 93% of communication is non-verbal, and has a deeper effect on self-worth than mere words. A great deal of information can be communicated through a simple gesture or facial expression. I can recall as a child being alert and ready to run based on a harsh adult tone of voice.

Developing the ability to associate meaning with non-verbal forms of communication begins from the moment a child is born, and continues throughout the stages of childhood. We form our expectations for physical survival and for emotional connectedness through these cues from our role-models.

We are, above all, born emotional beings. We have a natural ability to learn to navigate our circumstances by using our five outer senses and also our inner senses, called emotions. Children are naturally feeling beings. They express themselves in the moment, no matter what the emotion. When things happen, they feel the emotion, release it and move on. Go to any park and watch children interacting. Watch a child as it falls down and looks around to see if anyone is looking. The child is gauging whether there is a reason to be upset. If not seriously hurt, the child will get up and resume playing, or there may be a few genuine tears. This demonstrates that children are not conditioned to react. The child feels something, perhaps the shock of the fall, and when it senses that there's nothing to be upset about, the feelings moves through quickly and they return to being happy. However, add in a parent who comes running in panic, and the child begins to cry as a way of getting attention and / or because it has absorbed the parent's fear. If the parent continues to react to the child's falls in this way, then the child will become conditioned to react with crying, even if there is no real need to cry. Watch two kids fighting and they will yell and scream, perhaps scratch, or bite, but three minutes later, once the emotion has subsided, with or without intervention, they are playing well together again. What I am trying to illustrate is that children express in the moment. They don't hold onto emotions.

If we go back to the little girl whose father told her she was stupid, although she may have felt it was untrue, it created space for confusion and doubt. Her perception of the event (caused by a thought and a feeling at the same time) was that she was stupid, simply because her need to believe her father was greater than her self-knowledge at this point in her development. Given that belief in her father, there was no chance that the child would believe that she was good enough just as she was. When children feel they are lacking, they attempt to please in order to prove otherwise and gain approval.

It breaks my heart listening to clients relive this confusion at not being good enough. It's heart-wrenching to see the fear that they will never be good enough for love, for success, or for happiness, relived. They may be only perceptions, with no basis in fact at all, but what we believe tends to be realized.

To understand this, we have to understand the Laws of the Mind and how the mind assigns function. We need to understand that we have a thinking mind, and an emotional mind, and how that makes us form perceptions and beliefs, many of which are not true.

Notes:

> *"In oneself lies the whole world and if you know how to look and learn, the door is there and the key is in your hand. Nobody on earth can give you either the key or the door to open, except yourself."*
>
> **~Jiddu Krishnamurti**

CHAPTER 3

Mind Works 101

Our mind is made up of three parts, each with its own function and crucial job to do. For the purposes of the topic of this book, we will not cover the primitive mind (third part), as it has little bearing on the subject:

CONSCIOUS MIND / CRITICAL MIND *(think of this as the tip of the iceberg)*

- 5% of the mind
- Thinking mind
- Rational, analytical, logical
- Role is to make sense of our world
- Uses our senses to interpret information
- Faculty that uses willpower
- Short-term memory

SUBCONSCIOUS MIND *(think of this as the mass of the iceberg below water level)*

- 95% of the mind
- Emotional, feeling mind
- Role is to protect our beliefs
- Non-judgmental
- Responds to imagery using all senses, both outer and inner
- Permanent memory storehouse
- Protects our belief, value, and moral systems
- Single most goal-oriented mechanism known to man (told you that you'd hear this again!)
- Acts below the level of awareness

Any message is composed of three parts: the verbal content, the non-verbal content, and the state of mind of the receiver of the message. The verbal part refers to the words and their definition. The non-verbal part is the sum total of the speaker's gestures, body language, and tone. As stated in the previous chapter, 93% of communication is non-verbal.

Take the example from Chapter 2, when the mother calls her son 'a bad boy' when he breaks his grandmother's vase. Without knowing the non-verbal part of the comment, the child must take it at face value. 'Bad boy' are words he can understand. By the age of two or three, a child will have learned verbal communication and will have begun to learn about his / her world through words. However, if the comment is made and there is a smile on his mother's face, he may believe that his mother is not angry with him, only mildly reprimanding. If the comment is made in a stern voice, with angry body language, the child may believe that his mother is truly angry and that he is, indeed, a 'bad boy'. Children are more affected by the tone of voice and body language than they are by the verbal content. Based on their interpretation of the verbal and non-verbal content, they decide how they feel about the comment.

Thought + Emotion = Perception

In our modern times, information is flowing to us at Mach Three. The radio, television, the Internet, newspapers, and magazines provide information all day. We also receive information from the people we associate with in our daily lives. This information enters our minds via the conscious mind, and guess what - there is no stop button. So the conversation of the teenager sitting behind you on the Skytrain yattering away about the party she went to on the weekend is making its way into your mind! This happens even if you're not deliberately eavesdropping (well, maybe a little).

Our mind receives and screens information through the five senses: touch, taste, smell, hearing, and sight, and interprets it. Every day, from birth, we are responsive to our environment and we take all kinds of information into our minds. As early as infancy, we can tell whether it's cold or hot based on sensing the temperature of the environment we're in. We take this input in via our conscious mind. As children, we haven't yet developed the logical part of the mind. It hasn't formed yet, so there's no filter. Everything we perceive drops right into our subconscious mind, recorded for all posterity. Once we are able to rationalize, we use our critical thinking to analyze and evaluate an issue in order to form a judgment, but critical thinking isn't fully formed until we are adults. Logical thinking has to be developed to enable us to decide if input has value or not, and if it makes sense to us or not.

When asked the question "What kind of thinker are you?" most of us say we are logical or analytical. We believe that this is what makes us who we are because it's the only mind we are 'aware' of, but the largest and most dominant part of our mind is the subconscious, and we're generally unaware of it. The subconscious is our emotional / feeling mind, the part of the mind that stores all of our emotional memories from the birth of our awareness. It's like an organic computer that stores incredible amounts of data. Although our logical mind may seem to be the part in control, it's actually driven by the desires of the subconscious mind. And this, my friends, is the real us - and until we understand it, we don't understand ourselves.

Although we all have the ability to do anything we want, and are able to use our logic to aid us in making life choices, these choices are based on skills, experience, and willpower, which are aspects of our logical mind. Willpower is woefully short-lived. For example, you may really want to attend a social event, and your best friend is going with you. You know that you have the skills to navigate a social setting and the morals and knowledge to help navigate the social setting (getting blind drunk and dancing on the nearest table won't win you respect).

So why is it that you talk yourself out of going? Why is it that you can't seem to muster the courage to go, and the very thought of walking into the room makes you sweaty and nervous? Why is it that you suddenly get cold feet, feel inadequate, and scared? You don't know what the outcome will be, but you've already projected it - and so you go and hide in the closet. There's negative self-talk taking place and there's a feeling driving that thought.

Thought + Emotion = Perception = Belief = Actions

When we felt sad, angry, or happy for the first time; those feelings found purchase in our mind. The feeling is coming from a belief stored in the subconscious mind. As human beings, we base all of our decisions on the strength of our desires and beliefs, and the subconscious desires and beliefs always outweigh the conscious ones.

An alcoholic may have the conscious desire to stop drinking, yet he continues to drink, even if it's costing him his family and his job. A bulimic may consciously and logically agree that stopping the behavior would make her happier if she could control it, but she continues to binge and purge as an emotional crutch.

This rationalization is a function of the conscious / critical mind. These people can consciously accept the benefits of confronting their addictions. They may set in place all sorts of strategies to change: dieting, AA, self-help books, etc., and use their willpower to put things in action, but, again, willpower is short lived. It works for a while, like an indulgent parent giving a child a bit of leeway. Here's the kicker. Unless the subconscious mind agrees on a desire and directs its energy to that desired end, the change won't happen. No amount of conscious willpower will override the subconscious mind. The subconscious doesn't work from logic, but emotion, and the emotion is in the driver's seat. If what you want to accomplish logically is in conflict with an existing belief, it will not be subconsciously accepted. It makes no difference if the belief is good or bad for you. The subconscious just protects it.

Until the age of eight, there is very little logical function developed in the mind. Before this age, children use perceptions of their environment as well as observation to understand their world. The task of the logical mind is to make comparisons between what has already been repetitively learned. Before eight years old, everything is very new. Everything we learn is by perception, and how we feel about the things that we perceive will form a belief. We all program our beliefs by misinterpretations of events, and the opinions and beliefs of our role-models, who were in turn poorly programmed in their own early years. As we learn new things, the conscious mind accepts them, and without developed logic, they are dropped straight into the subconscious mind. Voilà, a belief is formed, and the subconscious mind accepts it, without judgment. The subconscious doesn't care if a belief is true or false, and it then begins the job of protecting that belief. Once a new idea is planted, it becomes the absolute truth for the person for life. The subconscious will then use that belief to evaluate all future ideas, and behind the belief is a feeling. Whenever there are events that trigger the feeling around a belief, it compounds it and makes it stronger.

When the logical part of our minds is fully formed in adulthood (between the ages of 25 and 29), the conflict really begins. We all formed false beliefs as young children. For example, if our mothers taught us repetitively that a square was a circle, we'd believe it. Come kindergarten, we'd learn from the teacher that the square is a square. Yet we would be confused and then challenge that idea because it's not what we learned. We would have to relearn a habit ingrained over time. As adults, we are able to rationalize new ideas and information coming in from the conscious mind. The conscious mind now uses logic to evaluate and compare each new idea with previously accepted beliefs, which are firmly planted in the subconscious mind. If the conscious 'mind 'changes its mind' after something has been subconsciously ingrained, the subconscious will not change with it (note: the subconscious can be reprogrammed, thankfully, with time). When we consciously set goals for ourselves to change something, our subconscious mind needs to support that. The subconscious will continue to dictate our desires and actions / behaviors in spite of our conscious opinion until there is congruency between what you logically think an what you subconsciously believe. It will not accept anything that doesn't support the beliefs already stored there.

Let's look at the career promotion example again. The conscious logic accepts that a promotion is possible, but the subconscious mind may have a contrary belief that you don't deserve success. When the logical, thinking mind compares its acceptance that getting a promotion is possible with what the subconscious mind holds as a belief regarding success, if that subconscious belief does not support the conscious thought, then it will be rejected. The subconscious will override your conscious logic in favor of its belief in any area of your life. It could be success at work and / or in your relationships. Why? Again, because the one job of the subconscious is to protect the original belief and drive the behavior that supports it without judgment. What happens next is so often the theme underlying all my work...self-sabotage. Where there is strong feeling around a belief, it will override the thinking, logical assessment every time.

I've had women who come to me who are dejected, beaten down, and at the end of their rope. They come from all walks of life, all income brackets, and all social levels. The common theme is that they desperately want to change, they want to feel peace and happiness, yet have not found a solution. They find themselves perpetuating behaviors such as picking abusive partners, staying in dead-end jobs, eating too much, drinking too much, or smoking too much. They all believe they lack the self-confidence and the willpower to change because they've tried and failed. If they had those elusive qualities, they would be happy and peaceful...and successful.

I remember an Oprah show years ago on the topic of self-change. The analogy of a pothole in the road was used to illustrate how we continue unhealthy behavior.

You are walking along, thinking your thoughts, and suddenly you fall into a big pothole. It's dark and mucky and you feel disoriented, but after a while you realize what happened. You climb out - with difficulty, perhaps a bit bruised, and continue on your way.

The next day you are walking down the same road and fall into the pothole. You now immediately recognize what happened and find the way to get out, having collected more bruises and scrapes. This goes on for days, or even weeks or years!

Then one day you walk down the same road and see the pothole up ahead and remember that it wasn't a fun trip. So this time, you walk around it!

Even though falling into the pothole is hurting you, whether the pothole is a bad habit or a perception, sometimes you just can't see it - or you can't seem to see a way to get around it. It's like tunnel vision. So you walk and fall, over and over again, until you're bruised and bleeding, sometimes even choosing to stay in the pothole because you have no energy left to haul yourself out. Been there, done that. So why do we do it?

It's because it's what we know. It's what we believe we deserve. The hard path we've learned. The subconscious mind is habitual. It's all about security, and security is not about pleasure. It's about what's familiar. We come to believe, after so many attempts to overcome our challenges, that there is no other path, just the one with the potholes. The potholes ahead may be larger and deeper, or smaller and shallower. It doesn't matter. We can hope for the shallow ones, but the fact remains that we feel there's no choice but to keep falling in and clawing out again in the hope that somewhere up ahead is a freshly-paved stretch of road. Human beings are programmed to survive. Security is that which is familiar, but is that all we want for ourselves? No. We are evolved, and since the first human our needs have grown tremendously, to include more than just warmth, food, sex, and shelter. With our curious natures, we have dreamed a future that we perceive gives us more; more opportunity to not only survive outside our tribes but to thrive as individuals. Yet how much happier are we today than 20, 50, or 100 years ago? From my vantage point, not much. Maybe it's time to look again at our lives and get off the merry-go-round that has us stuck in our ruts.

The logical mind is pretty much at the mercy of the subconscious mind. It's rational, not the part of us that drives thought, feelings, and the accompanying habits that dictate our rise or fall. The logical mind gets the messages from the outside before the subconscious mind, and if an incoming sensory message from the outside is not deemed in harmony with the established subconscious belief, the logical mind has no choice but to get rid of it. It's like shooting a BB gun at a brick wall. All the willpower in the world won't stop it from ricocheting back at the shooter. If we'd stopped and listened to ourselves as we made the decision to go for the promotion, for example, we might have heard that inner voice telling us that it was a bad idea. That we really don't have what it takes. We might have noticed the feelings that accompany the voice, such as fear, nervousness, anxiety, or sadness, but we soldiered on, due to willpower and the original thought that it was logical. Logical or not, the desired outcome won't happen if the subconscious mind isn't on board with the idea.

Notes:

> "Blessed is he who expects nothing,
> for he shall never be disappointed."
> **~Alexander Pope, letter to Warburton,
> Mar. 24, 1743**

> "I'm not in this world to live up to your expectations and
> you're not in this world to live up to mine."
> **~Bruce Lee**

CHAPTER 4

Blueprint of expectations

Like engineers, we all work from a blueprint, one that contains the history of all of our experiences all the way back to the womb. Within this blueprint is a series of expectations built from the foundation of our childhood bonding (or disconnection) with our parental role-models. No-one escapes this.

If we were raised with secure, loving patterns and expectations, we feel our own sense of worth in the world, and we subconsciously expect the same in our adult relationships. We navigate our lives, which are filled with all types of relationships, in a state of ease, rather than uneasiness.

When those patterns are cobbled together with threads of criticism, fear, and judgment, no matter how much or how little it is experienced in our early childhood, we perpetuate these effects into our internal blueprint of self-value. All infants are born with the instinct to bond with their caregivers, even before there is thought to apply to these concepts, or words to attach to the thought. Infants look for cues about their value through their connections with their mother and father, and their first impressions are through touch.

Infants sense through the arms of their parents whether they are safe or not, and it is internalized as an impression. When their sight is more acute, they look for favorable impressions through facial expressions. Smiles from their mother, funny faces from their father. Our need for attachment is a survival instinct. An infant's primal need for safely, comfort and connection is what makes them cry when their emotional or physical needs require attention. When those needs are met, the infant sleeps, or smiles, or coos to show they are in a happy place.

This tie that binds children and parents leads the infant to experience pleasure, joy, and safety…or not. Children look for comfort in their caregiver's arms. Our self-concept is shaped by our primary caregiver, and that is usually the mother. How our mother responded to our first cues for comfort, such as crying, influences how we expect to be seen by and responded to by others.

A baby feels distress when that primary caregiver is distant, whether physically or emotionally. Soothing, comforting, and providing pleasure, are primary elements of the mother-child relationship. John Bowlby (1907—1990), was a psychoanalyst whose evolutionary theory, called the Attachment Theory, suggested that children come into the world biologically pre-programmed to form attachments with others, because this helps them to survive. He believed that mental health and behavioral problems could be attributed to early childhood.

Self-esteem is a person's Teflon against the challenges of the world. When we lack it as adults, our insecurities are projected outward towards the world, casting everything in a dark net of fears. Our own insecurities present the world as an unsafe place, where no one can be trusted. We feel alone when we lack positive, nurturing relationships, and we sometimes become insecure and jealous when we're in a relationship because inside we don't feel worthy of love! We're hard-wired to belong, to have our physical and emotional needs met. This is the human condition. Without security, we are destined for loneliness.

I love the expression 'Our outer world is an expression of our inner world'. What we see outside ourselves is a projection of how we feel inside. Have you ever had a day where you were frustrated, and most of your encounters that day were with frustrated people or they brought out more frustration in you? We put our energy out into our environment, and like attracts like. We get what we put out there right back in our faces.

Security begins within. When we have a hard time bonding with others, we 'think' it's because of a lack in ourselves or in others, but I believe it's because we have lost trust in ourselves; trust in our ability to keep ourselves safe, or to trust that we will be safe, emotionally or physically, and it goes back to childhood.

Trust is seeded within ourselves. It's not something anyone can give us or sell to us. Our subconscious blueprint drives us toward seeking a tribe. When the world is perceived as dangerous, we tend to run or hide from relationships. I think all of us want healthy relationships, and that's both logical and a right. There's a plethora of easily available reading material about how to have beneficial relationships with lovers, friends, co-workers, and supervisors, but what drives our behavior is not found within the pages of a book.

Our subconscious, goal-seeking mind dictates our success in forging deep, long-lasting and loving connections. Because the subconscious is simply a goal-seeking mechanism, it doesn't analyze or rationalize all the self-help advice. It will take in only that which is in harmony with its internal beliefs. It's programmed to base all of our actions on our profoundly-rooted belief systems about ourselves. If what we want consciously is not in harmony with our beliefs, it will be kicked out the door. If the program is one of lack, where the primary self-perception is that we are unlovable, based on events from childhood and compounded through life experiences, then without intervention to rewrite the program, the subconscious mind will continue to create what we believe we deserve into our experience, which inserts a condition ripe for drama into our relationships. Changing the program is the key to changing self-beliefs, not what's right or wrong, or even who's right or wrong.

In order to help my clients, my partnership with them has been to help them move towards healthy, organic relationships, and to rewrite their early blueprints in order to change their self-perception from one of self-doubt and unworthiness to one of personal intrinsic love, and to promote a return to awareness of self-value, which is a birth right. It involves putting the feelings and thoughts of the child mind, which still holds all hurts, into words. The childhood perceptions of self are the program which the subconscious mind protects. The reframing of early root experiences enables them to have closure, to finally make peace with their early role-models, and most importantly, with themselves. This reframing process also educates the mind by providing an understanding that parents are never perfect and react only from their own internalized beliefs and their personal childhood experiences, and that it was never the child's fault when they were reprimanded verbally, physically, or both. Their behavior was normal for a child and they were not unlovable.

Once a client reaches this level of healing, their perspective towards relationships changes, and allows for new relationships to develop, even with those my clients are currently involved with, such as a partner, child, friend, parent, sibling, or co-worker. There was no change happening in the client's exterior world. The relationship shift is internal. 'When you change the way you look at things, the things you look at change'.

Within the experiences of your life so far, you may see patterns within your life blueprint. What are some of the patterns you notice interpersonally (socially, with friends, romantically, or professionally)?

Notes:

> *"Your intellect may be confused,
> but your emotions will never lie to you."*
> **~Roger Ebert**

> *"The deeper that sorrow carves into your being, the more joy
> you can contain."*
> **~Khalil Gibran**

> *"Feelings are much like waves, we can't stop them from
> coming but we can choose which one to surf."*
> **~Jonatan Mårtensson**

CHAPTER 5

How emotions drive our thoughts and actions

I remember as a child, whenever I did something perceived as wrong according to an adult caregivers' measuring stick, I was called stupid. In Portuguese, which is my first language, it was a heavy word, with room for accentuation. *Stupidaaaaaaa*! It hurt like heck. It caused me a lot of confusion, because I didn't 'feel' stupid. I did lots of things right, and my teachers all thought I was smart. They affirmed this with verbal praise and smiles, in ways I understood. I knew this by Grade 2.

A pivotal point for me was Grade 3. This was when 'stupid' became rooted as a belief, with tendrils kilometers long, and although I was aware of it from my own adult self-talk, I discovered the root through working with my hypnotherapist.

I was eight years old and my parents, immigrants, were making their first trip home to Portugal in many years. I'd never been there, as I had been born in Canada. It was end of November. Due to the cost of four airline tickets, my frugal parents decided we would go for two months to make it worthwhile, and stay over Christmas. I took the homework I'd be missing with me, and diligently ensured I did all the assignments and reading while away. I felt confident that I'd be good to go when I returned.

Within a few days of my return to school in late January, I was sitting at my desk towards the back of the class watching my beloved teacher giving a lesson, and I realized in horror that I didn't know what the heck she was talking about! It was as if she had suddenly started speaking another language. I can still remember the sensation I felt in my chest and stomach of getting so anxious. I was so worked up I threw up all over my desk and the floor - and mixed in with that mess was my self-worth.

I lost my confidence that day along with my breakfast. In fact, at the end of the year, although I passed to Grade 3, I was put in the 'special' class. For me, the foundation was now set for my lack of self-belief. I had been called stupid by those I trusted enough times to compound the perception as truth, and I now perceived that my Grade 3 teacher, another important role-model, thought I was stupid as well - for why else would she have recommended me to go into the 'special' class (which, by the way, was a wonderful year that rebuilt some of my confidence in my school abilities)?

The belief that I was 'stupid' became like a shadow, following me everywhere for many, many years. Whenever I did something I felt was wrong, my inner critic always responded with 'That was dumb', or 'How could you be so stupid?' It was a much smaller, more hesitant, and more confused voice that whispered from the depths of my soul 'How can I be stupid if I seem to accomplish good things in my life?'

Let's address the notion of emotions driving behavior. John Bradshaw, who wrote *Homecoming: Reclaiming and Healing your Inner Child*, stated, 'The primary motivating force in our lives is emotion. They are the fuel that moves us to defend ourselves and get our basic needs met (e=energy so emotion is energy in motion). Anger can move us to defend ourselves; to take a stand. We protect and fight for our beliefs, no matter how false they may be!'

Most people don't see emotion as a cause of their issues, or give their emotions much thought (I used to be one of them). They focus instead on observing and managing behaviors. We all have certain triggers – situations that cause us to have an emotional reaction and an accompanying physical sensation, and this triggers our primitive 'fight or flight' response. For me, that sensation has always been anxiety and a nervous stomach.

Unfortunately, whenever we are in an emotional state, it limits our capacity to think clearly, and causes us to move to ingrained habitual behaviors that aren't usually very effective or pretty to see. These emotions are triggered, and our habitual responses are driven, by our subconscious beliefs. For example, I worked with a client who responded with defensiveness whenever he felt criticized, regardless if it was constructive or not. Criticism was anything that made him 'think' he was wrong, and so was construed as a direct attack on his person, but what he was really feeling was that his game was up! To him, the criticism was validation that the 'criticizer' could see how imperfect and unworthy he was, and his automatic response was to fight back. He felt embarrassed at the thought of being judged, and he responded with anger.

Another client, when faced with the perception of criticism, reacted by retreating and hiding behind a wall that she would only peek around. She avoided difficult conversations, and justified it by saying that she disliked confrontation. She became a people pleaser. I love the saying that 'You're never upset over the things you think'. We get upset because of the way we feel. In uncovering the root of her issue, we learned that as a child, she would speak out of turn (what kid doesn't, right?)and be scolded for it. It made her sad that she had to be quiet. In her early teens, she tried to reassert herself by talking back when she had the courage to do so (passive-aggressive behavior), which led to disagreements with her parents, and punishment. So she smothered her voice again, good and deep. She would clam up and blush horribly when simply asked for her opinion at work, even if it was something simple, like 'what do you think of the new receptionist?' She didn't feel good enough to offer an opinion. She believed that if she was compliant, no-one would hurt her. If she was what others said what they wanted her to be, then she would be accepted, which for her equated to being loved.

Fear is one of the most toxic emotions that motivates behavior. 'What you fear you draw near' is a quote from Carolyn White, PhD. Many of us are too frightened to even imagine making changes to our lives. Again, security is that which is familiar. If we keep our job, our marriage, our life exactly as it is, then at least we know what we're dealing with. 'Better the Devil you know than the one you don't' is another saying that illustrates this point. We resist change, because we will do almost anything to avoid physical and / or emotional hurt.

To use an extreme example, how many of us have read about abused women who stayed in abusive relationships for years, maybe never having the courage to leave? We might ask ourselves 'Why the heck didn't she leave the first time he used her as a punching bag?' It's because the evil we know is better than the evil we don't know. The fear of the unknown is a powerful thing. These women are no different than any of us! What makes them do what we would not is their own state of self-worth, their internal beliefs about themselves, and the extremes they will go to in order not to be alone. If we feel we aren't good enough or worth much, then the punishment has to fit the crime.

When talking to groups about this issue of abuse, I use the example of a former client. She was a VP of Operations for a large corporation. She oozed chic and confidence. Even though I knew what her issue was from her intake forms, upon meeting her for the first time I did a double-take. Her story was that although she could handle corporate politics, oversee her department, lead a forty-person sales meeting composed 70% of men, and made a great salary, when she went home at night, it was to her husband taking out his frustrations on her physically. She used to avert her face when he came at her, because bruises would be harder to disguise.

Her internal belief was that at home, her husband was the boss. She submitted to his abuse because she had never been confident in her love relationships. She looked for love in her relationships, and respect for her from her partner was not as important. She had been neglected by her father as a child, and she came to believe that as a girl, she had no voice or value. Within her skill set as a professional, she found her voice. But in relationships, it was choked off.

We're all guided by our personal values, morals and beliefs. We all have some fractured form of self-value. When experiences have continuously battered that fragile part of us that knows we are worthy of being treated with respect and love, the belief that we are not only gets stronger. It's the law of compounding.

Unfortunately, it's the belief that we aren't good enough, lovable enough, and important enough that guides our choices, and the subconscious mind is in the driver's seat. It perpetuates that belief by having us search out the situations that match the belief, again and again, subconsciously and without judgment.

For example, think about choosing abusive men to have relationships with. If an abused woman were to look at her history, she would begin to notice that each relationship choice may have become progressively more abusive. Why? Because each abusive experience reinforced that woman's belief that she deserved to be physically and / or emotionally abused. She might begin to feel that she didn't deserve any better, not by conscious or rational choice, but because she believed that somehow, that abuse was her fault! The reason that she might feel this way is because of her inner child. That inner child came to believe, based on experiences in her early life, that if she had been better, more helpful, quieter, or perhaps invisible, she would then have been considered a good girl and have received the love, respect, and attention she deserved.

Another by-product of our feelings of inadequacy and unworthiness is the curse of perfection. When we believe that we're not good enough, or we're worth less than others (and believe me, there is not a living human being that doesn't share this belief to some degree or another) we subconsciously work very hard to be perfect. Society itself shoves it down our throats with television and advertising. Look at all the fun you have when you drink Budweiser. Notice how being thin has the men ogling as the tall, willowy woman walks down the street, flicking her long, lustrous locks.

We often believe that if we were perfect, we wouldn't be criticized, embarrassed, or fearful of being unmasked, and that would certainly make us happy. (Really? Not!) For myself, in my life, I created a world where I had control. I worked long hours to ensure that I had covered all the bases, and there wouldn't be any mistakes. God forbid I be called on an error. I'd rather have had needles stuck into my eyes.

Many people become controlling and aggressive when they feel overwhelmed. Others become self-absorbed, retreating into themselves. If a situation brings up feelings of fear, embarrassment, or anxiety, we react to those feelings in the ways we've learned to rely on (patterns of habit), and those reactions become habitual responses to stress. We may even find ourselves reacting as we saw our parents react when sad, frustrated, or angry. Often, trying so hard to be something we are not and failing at it compounds our feelings of inadequacy. (Vicious cycle, don't you think? We just aren't perfect, no matter how hard we try!)

We can't please everyone. Not even to save ourselves. When we're too focused on living up to other people's expectations, we aren't focusing on realizing what our own desires are. There will always be people who will judge us, talk down to us, or complain about us, but talk doesn't change or alter us in any way. Only acting on the things we hear can do that - and thinking about those things is acting on them.

This type of scenario brings to mind that childhood chant 'Sticks and stones can break my bones but words can never hurt me'. Guess what - it's true! The words only hurt if we let them. Recall the times you felt judged. How many of those times were simply your own perceptions, when your own expectation of judgment caused you to think you were being attacked because you believed you're weren't good enough? Did that nasty voice in your head tell you to fight back, retreat, or freeze?

By observing past events and asking ourselves if the belief behind them was true, we can find the beginnings of self-enlightenment. We'll begin to open our eyes to the perceptions and beliefs that we hold that really don't fit. We'll notice that they're old. For example, if we feel sadness at not being good enough, and that feeling doesn't match up with what we know to be logically true (we really don't have to prove anything to anyone), question the feeling, the source, and the situation.

Asking these questions works in two ways:

1. It helps you identify what those negative beliefs are, and
2. You can then start the process of creating new, healthy beliefs that become your revised blueprint in life, by which you are no longer so triggered by others' words or actions.

This process will help you see things differently the next time you feel judged.

If you want to gain self-awareness of the emotions that are driving your behaviors, you can start by asking yourself some of these questions when you are feeling emotionally triggered:

- What specifically was the trigger? (A person? A situation?)

- At the moment you felt triggered, what were you thinking?
- What emotions may be affecting you? (Sadness at not being valued? Disappointment? Anger at criticism? Frustration?)

If you can get in touch with the emotions that are driving your behavior, you've taken an enormous first step in self-change.

Notes:

"Unexpressed emotions will never die. They are buried alive and will come forth later in uglier ways."
~Sigmund Freud

CHAPTER 6

Suppression, expression, and release

The connection between your mind and body is very powerful. Science and medical studies show us that emotions have a direct effect on our health because the mind has a very profound influence on the body. When we're happy and have a good attitude, we create a more positive life and have a more positive outlook. When we have self-limiting thoughts and suppress our feelings by not dealing with our internal issues, we create an unhealthy life and outlook. Why? Because every thought has an effect on our physical self.

The subconscious mind stores our perceptions and beliefs based on our memories. When it senses danger in our external environment, it responds automatically to protect and defend against it. An event can trigger your memory storage house to release a negative or positive emotion, which will create negative or positive behavior, all based on your earliest perceptions and how you learned to react.

One of my clients was triggered every time her supervisor at work gave her feedback on projects she was overseeing. Although to anyone else it would seem that the supervisor was giving good feedback, all she heard was 'I messed up. I'm not good enough'. That automatic reaction was based on childhood memories of being told by her father that she wasn't doing it right, whether that concerned her homework, learning to tell the time, or learning to ride a bike. She responded automatically to the danger of being hurt emotionally, and her reaction was a blush blooming from her chest to her cheeks. Rather than being in control, she would lose control. Her ultimate humiliation was bursting into tears during one such incident, and that's when she found me. She'd stayed home from work for a week, unable to face her supervisor.

Dr. Gabor Mate, renowned author, speaker, and physician, wrote the book *When the Body Says No*. I jumped for joy when I read it, because here was a physician talking about the work I do every day! I found it illustrated well how, when we aren't taught to say no or to stand up for ourselves, our body will do it for us, and it's our own limiting belief systems that dictate how we respond to the world and how our bodies respond to our thoughts. Our feelings and thoughts have a direct impact on our physical states. As Dr. Gabor put it, 'Habitual repression of emotion leaves a person in a situation of chronic stress, and chronic stress creates an unnatural biochemical milieu in the body. Disease, in other words, is not a simple result of some external attack but develops in a vulnerable host in whom the internal environment has become disordered.'

Our emotions and experiences are essentially energy, and that energy can be stored in the cellular memory of our bodies. Think of a time when you experienced something really hurtful and you experienced the physical sensation of that feeling. For example, I can still recall the moment in 2005 when I suddenly learned that my youngest son might not make it through the night due to a brain tumor. I felt a sharp pain in my chest and the sensation of cold water being poured though me from my head to my toes. Afterward, whenever I was feeling deeply anxious, I'd get the same pain and cold sensation, and when I later observed how my body reacted to anxiety, I realized it wasn't new and that the 2005 event wasn't the root. It went back to a memory of seeing someone I loved strike another loved one in my presence. If you resonate with this concept, and you too have habitual physical responses to stress, it's likely because in some area of your body you still hold energy from a negative experience that is locked inside you.

When we have pain, tightness, or a hollow, empty feeling in certain areas of our bodies, we can find the emotional link inside ourselves. My clients have often thought I was crackers when I explained that their chronic shoulder pain was due to unresolved emotional issues causing that area of their body to react, wanting the issue to be addressed. The shoulders and upper back typically represent responsibility. Think of Atlas holding the world on his shoulders. The body is letting us know that the perceptions we are holding are too heavy. So, logically, this explanation will bring on a few eye rolls because we aren't in touch with our bodies or our emotions. We aren't taught to listen to our physical cues. We prefer logical explanations, but the truth is that our bodies do communicate with us. Chronic sore throats can often be traced to not allowing ourselves to speak our truth. Ear issues can be traced to the pain of listening to negativity, 'being told what to do'. The energy of the initial sensitizing event is still present in the body. If we address the subconscious emotions held in the body that are hurting us, we can lessen the pain and even heal it.

We use organic language to describe the things we don't like, the things that bring us pain, and we equate a body part to the feeling.

'My Boss is a pain in my neck', 'This fighting is making me sick', or 'It makes me nauseous to think about how embarrassed I was'.

The body is programmed for health, and it struggles with all the negative emotional energy we refuse to examine. Often, when we feel ill, pain, or nausea, it's our body's way of getting our attention. It's asking us to go inside, observe ourselves, and get it out.

Davis Suzuki wrote in *The Sacred Balance* that the condensed molecules from breath exhaled from verbal expressions of anger, hatred, and jealousy contain toxins. Accumulated over one hour, these toxins are enough to kill eighty guinea pigs. Imagine how toxic our body becomes after years of repressed emotions. We're walking noxious organisms!

Feeling our emotions is normal. We are human beings who emote in this theater of life. We aren't hardwired to hold in our feelings. That's a learned behavior. We learn to hold in our tears, our fears, and our anger because we were taught by our role-models and society that negative emotions and their actions are bad. I've had many clients, myself included, who found it was extremely difficult to cry. I'd rather have buried myself in a hole than let the waterworks happen! At the root, that's because we learned that indulging that behavior didn't bring us happy rewards - that it made us look weak. I myself heard 'Why are you crying? I'll give you something to cry about!' and out came the wooden spoon at Casa Rosa. Boys are taught that crying makes them look like a baby. Girls are taught that showing anger is unladylike. I'm not saying that parents today haven't come a long way from that, but it's still a perception that exists. Boys aren't encouraged to hang out in their rooms with their buddies playing with Bratz Dolls. Girls aren't often seen running through the yard with their girlfriends shooting toy guns.

Here's the truth. Our emotions were meant to be experienced in the same way we breathe. Feel them like an inhale, and then release them like an exhale. When we perceive those emotions to be harmful, or that they make us feel or look weak, we hold them in, much like holding our breath. You could hold your breath for about a minute, and it would be uncomfortable. After two minutes, it would be painful. After that, well, you'd want to exhale and take a breath, because your body would be panicking for that breath.

Our body holds all that intense energy of suppressed emotions, and it's not built for that. Our body's job is to stay balanced, healthy, and in a state of homeostasis, but because the body follows the mind, where the perception that feeling negative emotions is bad exists, the body doesn't have any choice but to store the energy. Over time, something has to give, and we become ill. Disease is the natural consequence of holding in unresolved feelings and issues. Our body enters a state of uneasiness versus ease. We develop physical and mental symptoms such as anxiety, depression, pain, or irritable stomachs. I came across a poster that said 'Crying is not a sign of weakness. It's a sign that you've been trying to be strong for too long'. Oh yes, I get it.

So holding our feelings in is self-sabotaging. In the book *Feelings Buried Alive Never Die*, by Karol K. Truman, she stressed that forgotten, ignored, or buried feelings are stored energy, and they have to manifest themselves sooner or later. We put on masks to hide what we think are our weaknesses, and we hide behind facades, all the while repressing our feelings so no-one can witness our pain and insecurities. We do it at work, socially, and in our relationships. When we think 'I have no idea what I'm doing, and now they're all going to know!', or 'You're going to disappoint him if you speak up', or 'I'm not that special', we are hearing our inner critic taking the stage. Take the microphone away!

- Suppression - holding feelings in
- Expression - feelings released without control
- Release - letting feelings out with conscious awareness

There is a way to work through suppression, but it takes some courage. The way to feeling better is through self-examination. Observing the feeling is already a step in the right direction - rather than have it come up and bite us in the ass. For example, take a scenario when we keep the feelings all repressed, and then something small makes us lose control in front of a friend, a co-worker, or a partner. Does that make us feel better after the dust settles? Likely not. Guilty, shamed? Likely so. This scenario is an example of expression.

Holding in the feelings doesn't make them go away. They're still there, under the surface, held down by our bodies. Imagine it as layers and layers of concrete that we poured in over the top of them, and without bringing conscious awareness to the feelings (being the observer), something beyond our control will let them loose! So why not practice releasing? The saying I think illustrates this best is 'What you can feel you can heal'. What we resist will persist…hurting only us!

It's healthy to cry when we feel it coming up - and why not scream in frustration? One key component here, though. Do it privately…duh! Not in the middle of the office, the yoga studio, or the mall. If we can observe it, we can control it till we get home or are in the car. We've already proven ourselves to be a master suppressors, so a few minutes or hours to find privacy won't take us over the top. If it's impossible to wait, we need to focus on the feeling that has us in knots, or bent over, and imagine breathing it out if we can't let it out fully in the moment. Imagine it like letting out some steam from a pressure cooker. Then, when we have the privacy, we can recall that moment when we originally felt the feeling and let it rip.

Once we have cried, screamed or pounded a pillow in anger (I highly recommend this one even though at first I thought it was silly), we will notice two things:

- Our bodies will feel better due to the release. We may feel calmer, more open, and lighter. We just created room for something good inside ourselves.
- Our minds will be clearer.

The thing about emotions is that they are energy. E in physics = Energy. So emotions are energy in motion. We need to move the energy. Ever had a frustrating day and then gone to the gym? Did you feel better? You moved the energy out.

Understand that the stronger the emotional energy, the less able we are to think clearly. Recall losing control. Were you thinking clearly when you shot daggers out your eyes and fire out your mouth???

Each of us has the capacity to be powerful by making negative thoughts and feelings powerless. Be open to change - and be open to the resistance to change!

What are your beliefs about being emotional?

When you feel emotion rising, what is your habitual way of dealing with it? Do you express, suppress, or release?

Write down an example of what that looks like. Example: *When I'm sad, I swallow it back and don't allow myself to cry.*

When you feel sad, you_____
When you feel anxious or nervous, you _____
When you feel angry or frustrated, you_____
When you feel bored, you_____
When you feel scared, you_____
When you feel confused, you_____

The next time you feel these emotions, which you will, notice where you are feeling the emotion in your body. Just observe it, without judgment. If you can, take it a step further and ask yourself what the emotion is that's causing the physical sensation. We don't often identify with the emotion enough to describe it. We come up more easily with the sensations of emotions using descriptors such as pain, pressure, and tightness.

Then ask yourself if you have had any problems, issues, or illnesses in that area. For example, I worked with a young woman who had TMJ Disorder in her jaw (the temporomandibular joint is the hinge that connects the jaw to the temporal skull bones). Whenever she felt anger or frustration and suppressed her voice, she held that emotional energy in her jaw. It was as if her body was preventing her from speaking because ultimately she was afraid of what she might say. Interesting and amazing!

Notes:

"When you are inspired by some great purpose, some extraordinary project, all your thoughts break their bonds: Your mind transcends limitations, your consciousness expands in every direction, and you find yourself in a new, great and wonderful world. Dormant forces, faculties and talents become alive, and you discover yourself to be a greater person by far than you ever dreamed yourself to be!"

~Patanjali

CHAPTER 7

Participant, observer, creator

What is participant observation? The definition of a participant is a person who takes part in something, and observation means receiving knowledge about something by watching it.

Participant: We are like a soldier in battle. All we see is what is in front of us, and we react emotionally and physically to outside stimulation / environment.

Observer: We are like the general, higher up on the hill, looking down at the battle. From this vantage point, we can see the patterns, situations, and the full conflict.

From observations, we can see what is happening on a larger scale, and then record these observations to help us decide if what's going on is creating a positive result based on our desired outcome, i.e. opening / achieving / gaining ground.

Creator: When we become the creator, we can take all the information from our experiences and create a new plan, with strategies to achieve the positively desired outcome.

It's a step-by-step process. We can't create without observing what we've been participating in. We need to achieve a clear understanding, and that comes from observing behavior to allow for ideas to flow in the creation of something new.

Let's look at the analogy of the butterfly lesson.

One day, a small opening appeared in a cocoon. A man sat and watched the butterfly for several hours as it struggled to force its body through the little hole. It appeared that the butterfly had got as far as it could, and it could go no further. It seemed to stop making any progress.

The man decided to help the butterfly. He took a pair of scissors and opened the cocoon. The butterfly then emerged easily. But it had a withered body; it was tiny and had shriveled wings.

The man continued to watch, because he expected that at any moment the wings would open, enlarge and expand, and be able to support the butterfly's body, and become firm. It didn't happen. The butterfly spent the rest of its life crawling around with a withered body and shriveled wings. It never was able to fly.

What the man did not understand was that the restricting cocoon and the struggle required for the butterfly to get through the tiny opening were nature's way of forcing the fluid from the body of the butterfly into its wings so that it would be ready for flight once it achieved freedom from the cocoon.

Sometimes, struggles are exactly what we need in our life. Although there may be well-intentioned people who want to help us, our paths are our own. It's our journey. So what does the analogy of the butterfly mean for us humans?

The cocoon can represent our perceptions about ourselves and our lives. The power of our thoughts can create a perception of what we believe our world to be...either a prison or a classroom. In the prison, we only see the hurts, the lacks, and the frustrations, and we project them out to the world because it's their 'fault' that we're in the prison. Although we don't look in the mirror for our part in it, we participated in events that were harmful to us, and we continued to do so because this is was what we knew. In the classroom, we observe, learn, and have the opportunity to create. The beauty of this is that thoughts never leave their source, and we all have the capacity to choose what to think and do. We can either evolve and become amazing human beings, based on our personal definitions of what that is, or metaphorically 'wither away' in a prison surrounded by bars we ourselves created subconsciously.

Sometimes, our experiences require us to go into a 'cocoon' to rest or retreat before emerging again. This can be therapeutic. For some, it's a time of observation, and for others, it's a pity party. I've experienced both, and licking my wounds was a necessary step in my healing. The self-imposed rest can permit us to go inside ourselves to ask the tide-turning questions 'Have I had enough yet?' and 'What have I been doing / thinking / feeling that's contributed to where I am now?'

We may think that we're doing the right things to make changes, but we may really be chasing our tails, or going through the motions and believing that we're going somewhere. We expect things to look different. I might get on a merry-go-round and see things as new on that first revolution but after that, every turn is much the same.

As human beings, we learn that security is that which is familiar. Familiar isn't always what's best for us. We prove this by staying in relationships, jobs, and circumstances that are toxic to us, but because they are familiar, the fear of the unknown keeps us prisoner within our own life experiences. When we recognize that we've had enough, and realize that we can't expect our efforts to produce a different result unless we change ourselves, that's when we can begin to emerge from the cocoon. That is the time we open to what and who we really are, and feel our worth. It comes only after the time when we sat in our feelings and our thoughts, in order to bring them to the light. It is only through feeling our emotions that we can connect to that part of us that guides our beliefs and values. The language of this habitual mind, the subconscious mind, is made up of feelings, metaphor, symbols, and imagery.

It may seem that we are alone when we emerge from the cocoon, having had to endure pain. I believe that our greatest lessons come from our greatest, deepest, most hurtful experiences. As beautifully said by the poet Anais Nin, 'And the day came when the risk to remain tight in the bud was more painful than the fear to blossom'. The process of opening ourselves to inner change doesn't mean that we can't reach out. There is no requirement that our growth be solitary. Yes, the process is one that we walk alone, but we can invite supporters to cheer us on at the sidelines. Our nature does not preclude us from receiving a helping hand, nor is it damaging when we seek help from those who care for us or when we get a helping hand from those who are trained to help with self-change.

If we went through our lives without any obstacles, it would cripple us. We learn by contrast. How would we know inner strength had we not felt weak? How would we recognize happiness had we never cried buckets of tears? It's the experiences of our lives that define who we are, and what we are capable of becoming. We wouldn't be as strong without our life lessons. Without them, like the butterfly, we would never be able to fly.

To face the hurts and obstacles we've experienced, and see them all as part of the journey of our lives that led us to be who we are right now, well, that's freedom. No-one can do that for us. As Iyanla Vanzant eloquently puts it, 'Every day is your day if you claim it. If you wait for somebody else to make it for you, you're going to be disappointed.'

Sometimes, a little extra effort is what gets us ready for the next obstacle to be faced. If we let fear, procrastination, or self-sabotaging beliefs hold us back from making the effort, or if we don't ask for help, we'll be left with our pants around our ankles when facing the next life hurdle that will surely come, and never manage to be free to take the leap to something better.

A good place to begin is to put on hold the behavior that's sabotaging us for a moment, and step back from being the participant in our lives who perceive we have no choices. When we do this, we can observe what we're doing. We can become more observant by asking ourselves why we're sabotaging ourselves.

Close your eyes and listen to your ' self' - and you'll begin to hear clues to why you do what you do. Take the first thought that comes into your mind. For example, it could be that you're afraid of going to a social event and it is scary for you. Begin with, 'I'm scared by the thought of...' and let the thought come. Repeat it a few times, because the first few responses may come from your rational mind, such as: 'I'm scared at the thought of being around new people.' OK. That's logical, because this is what you think is the reason. By the third try, it may sound like 'I'm scared at the thought of being judged', or 'I'm scared at the thought of looking inadequate'. The fourth time, you might hear 'I'm scared at the thought of not being good enough'. This is deeper than just being around new people. This is the subconscious 'why' to the feeling of fear and anxiety.

Doing this exercise puts us on the road to making more conscious choices to create what we **do** want in our life. A mind expanded never snaps back. Once we begin to become more self-aware, we can't go back to being a participant in the old way, because we know better. If we do find ourselves sliding back into participating, we can recognize it as a cop-out, because it no longer feels right. Once we know better, we occupy our lives better.

We can also read books to learn about emotions and how they affect us. I recommend *Feelings Buried Alive Never Die* by Karol K. Truman, and *Your Body Believes Every Word You Say* by Barbara Hoberman Levine.

We can keep a journal of our thoughts to work through anxiety, fear, anger, and sadness to get to the root issue. We can make lists of events where we self-sabotaged, and then write out what we did to self sabotage.

Noticing behavior brings it to our conscious attention. That, in turn, allows us to create a plan to begin practicing better habits. We can't change behavior until we're aware of it! Noticing helps us have more control, versus feeling mindless about what we say, think, and do. It's easy to point fingers and look outside ourselves for the answers to our angst, but the answers and the motivations for the behavior are inside us.

In a future situation where we feel we're starting to get triggered, as we likely will, we can watch our thoughts, and remain aware of the impulse to sabotage ourselves by saying 'That's interesting' (you're not engaging in the thought by just acknowledging it), take some deep breaths and let the thought pass away before we act. In that scenario, we're making ourselves the observer, and once we have control, we can create a different reaction that is healthier - and oftentimes safer - for us.

You can start right now, as you're likely thinking about it. Since we're all individuals, with our own stories and sets of perceptions, we can take a step to overcome self-sabotage by identifying how we sabotage ourselves.

Here's a space to begin. Go as far back as you can recall, and if you see a pattern, write it down. Use bullet points, or write out your answers.

Q1 – When I'm scared, how do I self-sabotage? (List events where this happened like turning down a date or a job offer.)

_____
_____
_____
_____

Q2 - When I'm anxious, how do I self-sabotage?

_____
_____
_____
_____

Q3 - When I'm confused or doubt myself, how do I self-sabotage?

_____
_____
_____
_____

Q4 - When I'm angry, how do I self-sabotage?

_____
_____
_____
_____

Q5 - When I'm sad, how do I self-sabotage?

_____
_____
_____
_____

Now, go deeper!

Patterns I see when I react, or pull inward emotionally (i.e. I'm afraid of leaving my job; I choose women who are controlling; I avoid social situations because I'm scared I'll embarrass myself).

Use the information you wrote in Chapter 4 about patterns.

_____

Notes:

Your mind is a garden, our thoughts the seeds,
You can choose to grow flowers or you can grow weeds.
The choice is yours, begin with a hoe,
Pull out those weeds, woe by woe.
And when you are done, be vigilant and true,
For what will grow is a beautiful You.
~Rosa Livingstone

CHAPTER 8

Critical self-talk - that nasty, 'dissing' voice in your head

Think about this...we have the ability to think 1,300 words a minute. Up to 70% of our mental chatter is negative. So imagine all the words you say to yourself in just five minutes that are self-deprecating! Self-deprecation is the act of reprimanding oneself by belittling, undervaluing, or disparaging oneself.

For many of us, it seems that being nasty to ourselves (putting ourselves down with our inner talk; abusing our bodies) comes far more easily than loving ourselves. If, like me, you've mentally beaten yourself for years, trying to get that miserable, bad-omen-portending inner critic to shut up, you're just on a merry-go-round of emotional misery.

I flinch when I think of all the nasty, hateful things I've said to myself over and over until they became the Habitual Response Team that arrived at every event in my life. I've spent many hours caught in a mental loop of self-flagellation at my mental whipping post, all caused by my ego trying to justify my sense of lacking something.

It sometimes feels too hard to practice self-compassion. Compassion towards others has always been a cornerstone of my being, but compassion towards myself — that's a heck of a lot harder. It's a battle I don't want to participate in. I have to choose to walk away from my inner fighting over and over again, every time I slip. But it become easier over time with awareness.

We speak to ourselves in ugly, condescending, and ridiculing ways. We say things like 'You're so stupid', or the variation I heard myself say so often, like 'That was so stupid'. You might hear, 'No wonder no one listens to me', or 'I'll never be happy', and 'I hate myself'! If we stopped to listen to our own negative inner voices, we'd find that it doesn't think much of us. The crux of the matter is that it's us creating this nasty dialogue. Even if we shoot the blame out to others, like our partners, our parents, our bosses, our friends, it doesn't solve the problem. It may bring us some relief in the short-term, but in the long term, the venom remains.

Thoughts create feelings within us, and the thought is rooted in an original, long-ago feeling and thought that we experienced that formed a negative perception. A constant barrage of malicious and vicious inner bullying doesn't leave us feeling warm and fuzzy. And given that we learn by repetition, or compounding, the more we think these thoughts the more they become our reality and the worse we feel. Oy vey! Or as my Gramma used to say, 'Ai meu Deus!'

Consider the quote from one of my favorite authors, Louise Hay, which sums it up perfectly: '...if you don't have the thought, you won't have the feeling. And thoughts can be changed. Change the thought, and the feeling must go.' Our inner voice is only echoing something that we believe about ourselves, but it's not in alignment with our true selves. That voice is reaching up without judgment from the depths of our own subconscious mind, the protector of our beliefs! The subconscious doesn't sit there and evaluate what it brings to your consciousness through your feelings because that's not its job. Its job is to protect what you came to believe with powerful and ruthless efficiency. It's really important to keep in mind that what that inner voice says is not the truth. No child is born that isn't worthy of life, of love, of joy, of validation, but something happened in all of us to change that. An event or a situation that planted a seed that was false, But a child doesn't know any better. What gets in first sticks and is planted deeply and boy, the roots become thick over time.

We must choose not to be our own worst enemy. We do need to stop and listen to that inner voice, because therein lies an opportunity to ask ourselves 'Is that really my truth?' Or, to ask ourselves 'Would I say what I say to myself to my best friend?' Here's another opportunity to begin a healing journey to re-write the script playing within us. It's only in recognizing what's behind those hurtful words that we can choose again what we feel about ourselves and how we want to treat ourselves. As children, we didn't have that choice about how we interpreted events and feelings. The constant mental haranguing that we experience daily becomes so habituated that we don't even notice we're doing it. Start noticing!

We may even find that the voice in our head isn't our own. Maybe it's our mother's, our kindergarten teacher's, our priest / pastor /

reverend's voice, or our grandparents'. Do we want them stuck in our heads?

A good exercise is to write down these self-sabotaging strings of cruel words we hear about ourselves, and then immediately write down the positive opposite. I've provided some space below to start now. Read it out loud! Even if the positive opposite doesn't feel like the truth, 'fake it 'til you make it'. We've begun the process of feeding our minds something good and it does listen. Simply observing can bring our self-talk topics to the forefront. Sometimes 'I'm so stupid' can pass into and out of our minds so quickly we miss it completely. By being aware of it, we catch it more often and can do something about it.

A University of Madrid study[1] found that actually writing negative thoughts down on a piece of paper and then destroying them was effective. They recommended that we either tear them up, throw them in the trash, or burn them! The experience of physically getting rid of them helps reduce their toxic effects. Psychologists suggest doing this on a regular basis.

'Nobody can hurt me without my permission.' This quote from Mahatma Gandhi teaches us that we are in control. And I'd add that nothing can hurt us without our permission.

What we feel and how we react to something is always up to us. When we react to something that is said in judgment, or to something that we perceive is said in judgment, then whatever we think or feel is originating from our own insecurities and fears. It's our own lack of self worth that causes us to react. Not only

---

[1] *Treating Thoughts as Material Objects Can Increase or Decrease Their Impact on Evaluation*: by Pablo Brinol, Margarita Gasco, Richard E. Petty, and Javier Horcajo, 26/Nov/2012: http://pss.sagepub.com/content/24/1/41

does this apply to self-judgment (that nasty voice) but also to our reaction to other peoples' comments or opinions of us.

Remember, what other people say and do, or what we perceive / imagine they are saying and doing comes from the other person's judgments, based on their experiences, their childhood programming, their morals and their values. We have no control over that. We can only control our own thoughts, feelings and actions.

We all have free will. We have the ability to react to things or ignore them. Keep in mind that even if we think about something, that's reacting. It's giving away our power. I love the saying 'What others think of me is none of my business'. It's true! It's never about us, but our reaction is.

Take some time to note what your inner critic is saying to you, and how you can respond from a loving place. The responses can be used as a stop button when the self-belittling voice pipes up.

This may seem like a lot of work, but I bet you can come up with at least five. You should see my first list! More than five, I tell you. Try it now.

E.g. Inner critic says *'you'll never drive a nice car'*. Self-loving voice responds with '*I deserve to drive a car that makes me feel good behind the wheel*'.

Inner critic says: _____

_____

Self-loving voice responds: _____

_____

Inner critic says: _____

_____

Self-loving voice responds: _____

_____

Inner critic says: _____

_____

Self-loving voice responds: _____

_____

Inner critic says: _____

_____

Self-loving voice responds: _____

_____

Inner critic says: _____

_____

Self-loving voice responds: _____

_____

Notes:

> *"You yourself, as much as anybody in the entire universe, deserve your love and affection"*
> **~Buddha**

CHAPTER 9

Negative influences that cause us to self-sabotage

Our pain didn't just appear out of nowhere. It was forged over time by the fires of misperceptions and by bruising to our souls. What we first learned about ourselves stuck, and it became the basis for who we think we are today. Whatever happened to us to hurt us was real and we don't have to try to validate it. The only thing that needs validating is how we perceived the events and people who hurt us, and perception is not reality or fact.

Here are some of ways we may have been wounded in the past and how they are damaging us today with self-sabotaging thoughts and actions:

Rejection

In childhood, our needs may have been rejected in evident or overt ways. Maybe we felt rejected when a new sibling was born. Or perhaps we felt it when we were compared to a sibling, a cousin, or someone that we took to be better than us, and that led to hurt and a feeling of loss of love. It left us feeling as if something were missing inside us that caused love to be pulled away, and it left us with the thought that we weren't good enough.

Rejection attacks the person we are inside. It leaves a crater where self-love and self-esteem should exist. It leads us to question our purpose and carry unresolved emotional wounds around like heavy boulders.

Whenever we experienced rejection in our adulthood, we questioned our value. It could have been that we weren't chosen for a job we were shortlisted for and we desperately wanted it. It could have happened when someone we liked or loved chose someone else over us, and as a way to protect ourselves, we may have built thick walls around ourselves to keep at bay the fear of rejection.

Abandonment

Much like rejection, abandonment strikes to the core. It severs a bond between us and someone we loved or cared for. There are many things that can make us feel abandoned. It may have appeared in our lives when our parents divorced, when an older sibling moved out of the family home, and when a childhood friend moved to another school. It may have shown up when our parent or parents didn't fully support, understand or communicate with us when we needed help, consideration or safety.

I've worked with adults who were adopted as infants; while consciously they didn't feel their adoption contributed their issues, their secret selves held the belief that if their parents could give them away, then they had no value and were unworthy of love.

These situations can cause huge emotional pain and affect our ability to trust others and ourselves. It hits the bulls' eye on causing lack of self-worth, and it creates issues in bonding with other people for fear they will leave us.

Embarrassment/Humiliation

These are twin issues. Any time we've been embarrassed or ridiculed, we felt humiliated, whether the ridicule happened in front of others or not. Maybe a parent called us stupid, or said something like 'you never do anything right'. Maybe we were a ridiculed by a teacher in front of the class by making us read out loud and then criticizing our delivery. Maybe we were bullied in the school yard and being called fat, or ugly, or dim-witted.

This brings up shame and guilt. We feel shame because something must be wrong with us, otherwise we wouldn't be made fun of or put down. The guilt comes in when we start to think that perhaps we did something wrong to deserve the brow-beating. Maybe if we'd put our shoes away like our parent asked they wouldn't have said we couldn't get anything done right.

Feeling inadequate as an adult is self-sabotaging, because we begin to doubt ourselves and hold back all the amazingness we have to offer. We develop anxiety at the very thought of being ridiculed that can turn into phobias. We never feel good enough to attempt more because we are so afraid of making mistakes.

Disappointment

Disappointment comes from failing to get what we wanted or needed, or even expected in childhood. A child who really wants a bicycle for his birthday and doesn't get one will be very disappointed. All our disappointment in adulthood comes from that internal space of hurt. It shows up when women are trying to conceive and aren't able to. It shows up when we really want that new 'thing' but can't afford it. It shows up when a friend has a party and we find out later that we weren't invited. That brings up rejection, abandonment, and a whole gamut of nasty feelings. Disappointment leads us to avoid situations so as not to get hurt.

Alternatively, we raise our expectations so high that nothing and no-one can meet them, so in the end we end up crumpled at the bottom of the stairs, feeling disappointed. This turns right back at us like a boomerang, making us the reason for being disappointed. We weren't good enough, smart enough, likeable enough, capable enough, pretty enough. We learn to distrust others because if we do, the other shoe is bound to drop.

Deception and Betrayal

"The saddest thing about betrayal is that it never comes from your enemies."

Deception and betrayal also leave deep scars. In childhood, we may have been lied to, like being told a family member was really sick but would get better, and then this person passed away. Maybe we were promised a reward that never happened. Perhaps, as in my home, there were secrets that could never leave the house, many of which I didn't understand.

I have worked with many clients who wanted desperately to learn to trust again after going through a divorce or infidelity in their relationship. I've had a few that were devastated by being passed up for a promotion when their boss had given every indication that they were a shoo-in.

The greatest deception and betrayal is when we perceive that we are unlovable because we were lied to, or betrayed by, the ones we put trusted the most. This really impacts our trust quotient. We learn to look at the world through eyes veiled with the fear of being let down, or deceived, or being caught off-guard. We ultimately start distrusting ourselves because our hearts were open, and then they were shattered, bruised, or cut out. This is self-sabotaging because we become afraid to give and receive love. We are always on our guard and want to control everything so that we are never, ever, ever hurt again!

Abuse

This one's hard for me as it was part of my early childhood experiences, and I have worked with many clients who came to me to heal the abuse they experienced as kids. It's not an easy task to hear their heart-breaking stories, and how they've survived many years with these horribly deep scars.

There are many types of abuse. Physical, emotional, and sexual abuse are all far too common in our world today.

We may have grown up in a home where we were physically punished a lot, or we witnessed physical violence from one parent to another, or from a parent to a sibling. Perhaps we were sexually abused by a trusted family member or a close relative or friend. Perhaps we were constantly put down, or made to feel small and helpless, or ignored and neglected. Maybe we felt that somehow the abuse was our fault. Maybe we still jump like a frightened cat whenever someone comes up on us unsuspecting, even though the intention was to give us a hug.

Abuse leaves more than physical scars. It's the ultimate trust-crusher. We then bring all our painful scas into our relationships. For some, these experiences sabotaged them as adults by having them endure being physically beaten, emotionally degraded, or forced to have sex when they didn't want to. This happens, even in marriage. It leads some people to be so afraid of being hurt that they walk on egg-shells and make themselves as invisible as possible. I'd wager that for all victims, it leaves them feeling like victims, with a crushing burden of guilt and shame.

A 2014 study, published in the Canadian Medical Association Journal, stated that 32% of Canadians had experienced physical abuse, sexual abuse, exposure to intimate partner violence, or a combination of these while they were young, and it includes punishments that were socially appropriate forms of discipline back in the day, such as spanking with an object, being physically thrown, or slapping.

This treatment can lead to a lot of mental disorders such as depression, suicidal thoughts, and even attempted suicide. It may lead to failed relationships, financial difficulties, addictions, and an inability to feel good about or take care of oneself. Some people bear an intense anger that they take out on themselves and others. Others carry so much fear that they develop debilitating phobias.

Any or all of these situations compounded our ability to forge healthy relationships not only with others but ultimately with ourselves.

Notes:

"Love yourself first and everything else falls into line. You really have to love yourself to get anything done in this world."
~**Lucille Ball**

CHAPTER 10

Some areas in life where we let our saboteur get in the way

Just as we can find countless ways to be happy and fulfilled, whether in our work, in our relationships, or in our social interactions, there are countless destructive ways in which we self-sabotage. It's back to the program, folks. We're unaware of the sunshine, or the possibilities available to us, because we're in the shadow place. If our subconscious discovered a way to protect us from the world or even ourselves, because the subconscious exists to protect us from danger, then it enforces the habit or automatic response to perceived danger, and this shows up in all areas of our lives.

If shedding weight is dangerous, then the subconscious keeps us from losing weight to keep danger at bay. The danger of being noticed might signal judgment. If meeting new people means we might be judged, ridiculed or embarrassed, then the subconscious uses anxiety to keep that danger at bay and away from social interaction. If leaving a codependent relationship means uncertainty and brings on self-doubt, then the subconscious uses fear to keep us in our circumstances. If connecting romantically might mean we could be rejected or abandoned, it uses sadness to keep others away.

There are so many parts of our lives that are affected by our in-held perceptions about the world and whether it presents danger to us physically and / or emotionally, far too many to cover here. The next five chapters are dedicated to the areas I see most in my practice. These areas represent where we screw up and where self-sabotaging feelings, thoughts, and behaviors are most destructive.

Using what you learned in Chapters seven and eight, ask yourself what areas you sabotage most your life. What do your patterns tell you? Can you relate these patterns to your childhood? Who may have reacted in the same way?

You are learning here about how you react to the triggers in your life, and how the beliefs driving how you react are not necessarily yours. You learned these negative, sabotaging behaviors by mirroring how your role-models reacted to their circumstances, as well as forming many of your own. Having information and relating it to yourself is a powerful step on the road to change. It strengthens your resolve to know yourself better.

> "I did then what I knew how to do. Now that I know better, I do better."
> **~Maya Angelou**

Notes:

"Crying is how your heart speaks, when your lips can't explain the pain you feel."
~Author unknown

"Only those that have known the dark places of depression can truly understand your sorrow."
~Rosa Livingstone

CHAPTER 11

Self-sabotage and depression

So many people suffer the effects of depression privately and silently. I did for many years. I know now that my journey along the dark landscape of depression began as early as six years old, and I really felt it in my 'tween years. At the age of twenty-three, I crashed, bewildered that I had 'lost control'. I had started a new, exciting career, was living in a vibrant city (having moved from a small town), and all of a sudden I was unable to cope. All I wanted to do was to hide under my covers and never get up, or cry my eyes out till they were swollen shut – and avoid having to face anything or anyone. The whole world was shades of gray, and I walked through my days putting on a happy face, which ultimately cost me even more of the precious little energy I had. I was bleeding internally where no-one could see. I kept it to myself, fearing that I would be labeled crazy, unstable, or too emotional or sensitive. I feared losing my job, my credibility, and even my friends.

I recall walking into a local hospital after work one late fall morning in 1988 and crying at the registration desk as I didn't even know how to tell the administrative staffer what I was feeling. I was almost incoherent. That began my foray into the world of psychiatry and medication.

Even with the major strides in society today, many people, including family members, friends, employers, and employees perceive depression as a stigma, and feel that it means the depressed person is unstable, imbalanced...mentally ill. I know that the most common statement given by the well-intentioned to clients who have come to me because of depression is that 'it's all in your mind'. Lo and behold, indeed it is. I learned that first-hand. However, it isn't something you can just talk yourself out of, or decide to stop doing.

Here are the cited statistics according to Health Canada and Statistics Canada:

- Approximately 8% of adult Canadians will experience a major depression at some point in their lives, and around 5% will experience depression in a given year.

- Depression continues to be Canada's fastest-rising diagnosis. From 1994 to 2004, visits for depression made to office-based doctors almost doubled. In 2003, that meant 11.6 million visits to doctors across Canada about depression.

- Rates of depression are especially high among Canadian youth. A nationwide survey of Canadian youth by Statistics Canada found that 6.5%—more than a quarter million youth and young adults between 15 and 24—met the criteria for major depression in the past year.

- In a 2013 survey of B.C. teens, girls were showing less improvement than boys in feeling distressed emotions. Of the almost 30,000 students who participated in survey of 60 districts, 17% of girls had contemplated suicide. Almost a quarter of the girls said they experienced depression, ADHD or anxiety attacks, and 13% of girls, compared to 5% of boys, said extreme stress had prevented them from acting normally. Girls are more likely to self-harm, with 22% reporting that they cut or injured themselves on purpose, compared to 8% of boys.

- 'Depression can affect children, seniors, and adult men and women of all socio-economic backgrounds', according to Ed Rogers, President of the Mood Disorders Association of BC. The stress of unemployment can make some people more vulnerable to depression, yet many people with depression also have prestigious and highly-demanding careers.

- Twice as many women as men are diagnosed with depression. However, this may simply be because men are less comfortable seeking help. They live with the perception that they've got to be strong.

Depression not only depletes you, but it depletes those closest to you. It's hard living with someone who is low, who has no energy, who just wants to lie in bed and hide from the world, even from those they most love. Depressed people can be hopeless, sad, negative, cynical, and overall, pessimistic. They're not fun to be around. I understand this personally.

Depression self-sabotages by casting a web of negativity around you, over you, behind you, and underneath you. It's like being trapped underwater. You see everything in a negative light; your work, your life, your family, and yourself. Often, you push people away because you don't have the energy to explain why you feel the way you do, and most likely you don't even know why you feel the way you do. You find loved ones avoiding you because you complain about how awful things are.

You may also suffer from anger and anxiety when depressed. The focus is on your feelings and not of those of others, and everything you see before you is bleak. When anger does surface, because you can't maintain any feeling for long periods of time, it's a way of escaping the intensity of the sadness. You swing from sadness to anger to anxiety, and back, with some periods of respite where you just feel numb. Depression isn't always about crying jags. It's also a defense against feeling sad, and feeling numb is like a holiday from the hurt. I used to think that at least when I felt irritated or angry, it pushed me to get up and get going. The anxiety for me was the fear of bursting into tears at work, and more deeply, of truly losing my mind. I seriously thought that I was going crazy, because even the simplest of tasks or decisions had me in knots. I couldn't make a decision to save my life at times. I was the 'walking dead".

Depression sabotages every aspect of your life, even if you manage to maintain a facade. It wasn't until 2006 when I was taking my Clinical Hypnotherapist training that I began to delve into my depression, and it scared me. Much as it hurt to go into all the sadness that had accumulated over years, I finally came to the place where I had excavated enough to feel freer. I had to ferret out the programs that I'd learned as a child that had me feeling so worthless. I came to the realization that depression hit when

I couldn't fake it anymore. It was my shut-down button when I just didn't have the resources to trust my own mind to guide me positively. With my self-observation, I was finally able to lower the voice that said I wasn't worth anything, so why try to prove otherwise. That was almost ten years ago, and was also when I took my last anti-depression pill. Yeah, me!

Symptoms of Depression:

- feeling worthless, helpless or hopeless
- sleeping more or less than usual
- eating more or less than usual
- having difficulty concentrating or making decisions
- loss of interest in taking part in activities
- decreased sex drive
- avoiding other people
- overwhelming feelings of sadness or grief
- overwhelmed when making simple decisions
- loss of energy, feeling very tired
- thoughts of death or suicide

If you suffer from a depressed state of mind or think you're depressed, try to find the courage to seek help. Reach out to a family member you trust, and if you can't do it, have them make an appointment with your doctor. It's serious stuff. Find a counselor, a psychologist or cognitive therapist, or a hypnotherapist.

If you feel you are depressed, or even find yourself feeling deeply sad a lot, or have been diagnosed with depression, here are some questions to ask yourself:

- How is depression self-sabotaging your thoughts and behaviors?

- How it preventing you from expressing yourself fully?
- What pattern do you see taking place?
- Do you play the victim (blame others for the circumstances that are making you depressed)?
    - If so, what do you need to do to choose to take responsibility for your feelings?
- Are you setting expectations for yourself that are too high for you to meet, which may be contributing to your feelings of sadness?
    - If so, how are they serving you?

Notes:

"Don't let your mind bully your body into believing it must carry the burden of its worries."
~Astrid Alauda

"Anxiety is a thin stream of fear trickling through the mind. If encouraged, it cuts a channel into which all other thoughts are drained."
~Arthur Somers Roche

CHAPTER 12

Self-sabotage and anxiety

If there was ever an age of anxiety, ours would be it. All of us regularly experience mild anxiety, but for some, anxiety escalates to overwhelming thoughts of doom and disaster, and even into full-blown, debilitating panic attacks. There are some for whom anxiety develops progressively over time; for others, it attacks suddenly, like a tsunami, and it's not a fun surf!

Anxiety is related to the fear of the unknown, and needing to control all aspects of our lives in order to be safe physically, emotionally, or both. Here's an acronym about fear that illustrates this perfectly: False Evidence Appearing Real. We get so anxious about the possibility of danger to ourselves that we act as if it's already begun. Often, anxiety is compounded by the fear of experiencing the anxiety or panic itself.

Our response to danger is a human instinct. It's the primal danger signal from our caveman days that gets our bodies ready to work up the energy needed to deal with threats to our survival. So what do we do when we're in danger? We only have three options: fight, flight, and freeze. If the threat seems smaller or weaker than us, we'll fight it. If it looks stronger than us, but not as fast, we'll run as fast as our legs can take us in the opposite direction. If it looks bigger, faster, and tougher than us, like a saber tooth tiger, we'll freeze and hope it somehow misses us - rather like how little kids cover their eyes and think they are invisible.

Extreme anxiety and full-fledged panic attacks causing obsessive thoughts or panic can be triggered by single event, or a series of events. They can arise out of our own experiences or from the experiences of others. Our response will be one of the above. It happened to me.

In 1992, while in the Paris Metro, I experienced a sudden onset of panic that made it impossible for me to travel on the subway. As soon as I saw the tight hallway slope downward, I couldn't breathe, and in my panic, I turned and ran back to the entrance, jumping the turnstile in Olympic fashion (I could have won the gold!). Once outside, I leaned against the wall and promptly became a puddle on the ground, crying like a baby, confused as to what was happening and overwhelmed by my actions.

The experience left its mark for several years, and it grew into feeling panic in underground parking lots, elevators, or any enclosed space. It became anxiety and fear associated to any place where I felt that fear come ripping up my body. At the time, I was bewildered as to what in the world could have caused this panic. Over the years, the symptoms did lessen, but the anxiety in situations of perceived danger still remained. I just didn't melt down. I coped by becoming more of a controller. Everything had to be planned out. Years later, I discovered that my panic came from a combination of my own experience and the experiences of another family member who was severely claustrophobic…my mother. I recalled her jumping a queue when visiting a grotto in Portugal and almost fainting in her panic to get out. Learning and working through what had caused my reaction was invaluable in dealing with the cause of my issues, and the symptoms literally disappeared quite quickly.

Anxiety and panic can be triggered by accidents, illnesses, or the deaths of friends or family members - incidents that suddenly thrust people into emotions they hadn't experienced so deeply before.

For some individuals, anxiety attacks have a sudden onset and sometimes go away as mysteriously as they began. In severe cases of anxiety or panic - those that don't just go away - the symptoms are grueling, while the true cause remains unknown. It can often appear that the particular incident that caused the panic attack doesn't justify the over-the-top response, and this is scary because we have no control, and the prospect of danger, which brings on anxiety, remains a threat because it's unresolved. Soon, the panic is sparked by the fear of the panic returning, i.e. we panic at the thought of panicking.

Some panic attacks are triggered by harmless incidents that symbolize a subconscious memory of an event earlier in a person's life. A truck driver suddenly developed a fear of driving through mountain highways or along rivers / oceans. This was really not a good turn of events for his livelihood, and it became so bad that he had to take leave from work. The fear was sabotaging him in a very serious way and impacting his ability to make a living.

By regressing him to the source of his panic, we discovered that when he was a small child, he had fallen into a pool. He was only one-and-a-half years old at the time, so he had no recollection of this event in adulthood. The fear he'd experienced at that event had become subconsciously imprinted, and his mind began protecting him from anything that was perceived as dangerous to his life. He'd inadvertently recalled this long-ago event when he was distracted and veered to close to the shoulder, where the drop led to a river. Although he tried to talk himself out of this 'ridiculous fear', the fear continued to take over and talk him out of driving near water. He subconsciously made a pact to never feel that terror again.

Once my client worked through this childhood event, he regained control, and the symptoms dissipated over a matter of months. He was also able to connect other self-sabotaging habits associated with this childhood event, such as his fear of not having control and his fear of taking risks. He once had wanted to take a sailing holiday with friends and had had to come up with a million excuses to avoid it and not look like a chicken.

I also once dealt with a client with severe obsessive compulsive disorder, or OCD. This compulsive behavior was linked to personal safety and fear of illness. The OCD compelled her to repeatedly wash her hands, up to fifty times a day. She self-sabotaged by trying to control everything in her life. She couldn't leave the house without checking that the lights and the stovetop elements were turned off, and that the door was locked (she checked this repeatedly before leaving). She couldn't go to a movie theater for fear of the seat being 'gummy' (her word). This led to social stigma (friends making fun of her), anxiety about social situations (had the waiter washed his hands before touching her plate or food when out dining with friends), and even anger at loved ones for telling her to get over it.

Whether in the recent past or in the distant past, some events leave negative psychological imprints. Sometimes they are forgotten or unrecognized, so we're left bewildered by the detrimental effects anxiety produces. Negative imprints can be left by traumatic incidents, but also by minor events that were misunderstood when they occurred. Those who suffer anxiety feel powerless to change, as most have tried everything to be 'in control' - and that's the kicker. We don't control our outside world. We only control our inner world. That's the world that can be changed.

- How does anxiety sabotage your thoughts and behaviors?

- How does anxiety prevent you from expressing yourself more fully (what do you fear will happen if you do)?

- What pattern(s) do you see taking place?

We need to look into resolving the deeper issue(s) causing the anxiety, but until then, there are methods we can use to minimize the effects of panic. Learning to belly breathe; formulating coping statements that we can have handy to help us through a tough moment, because it really is just a moment. Try something like 'I'm only having a panic attack and it will be over in three minutes if I breathe through it and relax' or 'This will pass, I'm safe'.

Notes:

> "Anyone who loves in the expectation of being loved in return is wasting their time."
> ~**Paulo Coelho**

> "The inner speech, your thoughts, can cause you to be rich or poor, loved or unloved, happy or unhappy, attractive or unattractive, powerful or weak."
> ~**Ralph Charrell**

CHAPTER 13

Self-sabotage, romance, and intimacy

Our critical inner voice reaches out to sabotage our most intimate relationships, even though those relationships are the thing we most want to be a part of. We want to be loved, protected, and feel safe in sharing our emotional and physical selves, but if our programming overrides trust in matters of the heart, we react with distrust, and anticipate or even expect rejection and abandonment. This makes it pretty hard to attract and sustain healthy relationships. So many clients over the years have had this issue intertwined in the areas they want to see change.

Perhaps we learned through our childhood environment that to be safe, we have to find someone to take care of us, because we felt abandoned and believed we were helpless. We then look for those relationships where our needs will be met. Our expectation of our partner is that he or she will fill all the voids, and that puts a lot of pressure on them. It may have them feeling that we're too needy, and have them running for the door.

If we've learned to be a perfectionist and control our lives so that we feel safe, because our childhoods was unpredictable, then we may look for a mate who we can mold into perfection, trying to change them, but we'll be disappointed because we aren't perfect, and nor is anyone else.

If we witnessed manipulation by our role-models, and / or passive aggressive behavior from parents or other family members, we will look for relationships where we have the upper hand, wear the pants, so to speak, so that we can avoid being challenged or made to look weak.

Inevitably, the very safety we're looking for, coming from a perceived lack, blows up in our faces. We get angry and defensive when a relationship doesn't work out as we expected. We tend to throw blame on the other person, e.g. 'It was his fault! I did everything to make this work!' or even blame ourselves with questions like 'Why did I let myself get involved with her? How could I have been so stupid?'. Our critical inner voice is defensive, and we use that voice most especially in love relationships. These relationships, whether with a lover, parent, best friend, or sibling, are closest to us, and the ones where we lower our guard. We think these people can't hurt us or that we can't hurt them because they love us or because we love them, but when something does happen to let us down, whether it was deliberate or not, the old way of reacting rears its bug-eyed head. We play out old behavior patterns with those we trust, and instead of being logical about what happened, we let our self-sabotaging shadow take the reins. We all project our inner hurts, lacks, and frustrations out into our exterior world as a way to avoid looking inside ourselves for the true root of our trail of broken relationships, or we turn to denial as a way of not dealing with our true feelings.

Let's look at distrust. If we felt abandoned as children, we may lean towards becoming insecure in our relationships, and the critical voice begins to pipe up, questioning why we let this person in. 'You can't let people in too close because they'll hurt you'. Your defense may be to run when someone gets too close. That was one of my go-to defenses. I used to say that in relationships I always had a good pair of running shoes at the front or back door.

Maybe our parent or parents were smothering and over-protective. This may lead us to feel smothered in a relationship. We need our space, and we protect it at all costs. We may come off as aloof, and our partner may rebel at not feeling that he or she is important to us, and when our partner asks more of us, the critical inner voice may say something like 'Get going, he's too needy' or 'I give enough already! Leave me alone!' We feel suffocated, and that leads to feeling trapped.

That misleading inner voice is just part of that goal-oriented mechanism that found defenses to keep away those people who potentially could hurt us the most, in our intimate relationships. We're afraid to be rejected, abandoned, disappointed, and saddened as we were as children, and will do anything to avoid those dark, heavy, painful feelings.

What's suppressed will at some point be expressed. Over time, physical symptoms can also arise from our self-sabotaging ways. We not only sabotage ourselves with our emotions, but damage our physical selves as well. So how do our feelings, thoughts, and actions based on our past affect us, specifically, in the bedroom?

Glad you asked. Did you know that your mind is the largest sex organ? This may be news to some who think that it's the nether-region 'junk'. Because the body follows the mind, it's the mind that dictates how your body responds in the bedroom like a Gladiator in the arena or clown at the stampede., and it can prank us really well!

Recall that the mind stores all of our past emotional hurts, whether they're related to romantic relationships (when our hearts were trashed by a lover who betrayed us / lied to us) or to familial relationships (not having felt loved by, or even having felt lied to by a parent as a child). The mind doesn't forget a thing! Yes, you've gotten that already from my repetitive coaching. Our minds protect us from re-experiencing those old wounds, without judgment, even when we're searching for love and think we deserve it...which we do, by the way. I see many clients in my practice who have challenges in the arena of the heart, some resulting in physical issues such as heart problems (really!) due to not feeling loved as a child, and having a parent or parents who did not demonstrate love either in words (saying 'I love you') or in actions (hugs, kisses).

In order for many couples to maintain a healthy sexual relationship, one or both have to work out their past wounds - to heal the mind in order to get their mojo up so they can be present in the physical and emotional act of sex. Because we are emotional beings, and our mind is the creator of emotions and communicates them to our bodies through sensations, it regulates our performance. If our mental blueprint includes not feeling good enough, sexy enough, good looking enough, the mind starts bringing up distractions, and that's not exactly a recipe for either intimacy or eroticism. We can try blocking out the voice and using fantasy as a way to stay in the moment, but it doesn't always work. Sex begins in the mind, and what it translates over to the body will either make sex fabulous and uplifting, or flat and depressing.

To illustrate the mind-body sex connection, I've had many clients who came to see me regarding erectile dysfunction. They were fine in the 'honeymoon stage' of a relationship, but once it became comfortable, difficulty arose (pardon the pun) in maintaining an erection. One client in particular attributed this challenge to the fact that he believed he was trapped after all the hot and heavy hormones slowed down. That's logical, but he was left feeling guilty about it.

In working together following his feelings of guilt and frustration (and shame, which we uncovered during the regression process), we came upon a memory from when he was eleven years old, of having sex with a thirteen-year-old girl who initiated it. She was his neighbor. My client felt confused and dirty, because he believed it was wrong and he was terrified his mother would find out. He was able to perform (even at eleven years old) but that shame and guilt were imprinted, and subconsciously he associated sex with being 'bad' even with someone he truly cared about.

Another client, in his early twenties, had the same issue, but it was because he was so afraid of 'doing it wrong' and being judged as a lousy lover. When we traced the feeling to his past, it had nothing to do with sex at all. It was his perception that he had to be 'da Man' because his father was always rewarding him for his masculine achievements, such as being a great fisherman or a great soccer player. The value placed on these abilities was part of his father's measuring stick. It didn't belong to my client. He couldn't be who he wanted to be for fear of disappointing his father.

Our mind has the ability to interrupt intimacy in a flash, often without conscious awareness. That can mean, for a man, that he can no longer hold his erection. For a woman, it can mean becoming less lubricated which can cause pain during intercourse. It can also happen due to outside forces, such as hearing a child call for you when they're supposed to be asleep.

We self-sabotage our romantic relationships emotionally as well. If someone has been hurt in the past, they may feel that all women are untrustworthy. This is a perception, not a fact, and will certainly lead to difficulty in making long-lasting commitments.

If we have been let down by love, it affects us on all levels. We may feel unworthy of love, emotional and / or sexual, and lead ourselves down the path of loneliness, or feeling desperate to find a partner. This unworthiness is also a perception but not fact.

Jealousy is another useless endeavor that rears its ugly head in relationships. It's a by-product of lack of self-trust. As we may have all done in the past, or may be doing now, we look for betrayal and conjure up all kinds of outrageous scenarios to support it. This is often caused by having been betrayed in a former love relationship and / or we had a philandering parent. It's a 'possessed state of suspicion'. We start imagining things that would justify our jealousy, and it spirals. Think of examples such as checking our wife's emails and texts, or going through our husband's clothing to see if there's another woman's perfume on his clothes.

Jealousy is centered around trust, and trust is one of the most fundamental aspects of relationships. Yes, if we've had cause to be jealous within our relationships, then the jealousy logically feels acceptable, but what if I said that our jerk of a past or current partner who fooled around on us is not at issue here? We are. We alone are responsible for our feelings, thoughts, and actions. We can't control any thoughts and actions but our own. What our partner did was about him or her, and not about us. We didn't do anything wrong. Suspecting a future infidelity is self-sabotaging, because we look for justification of our own feelings of fear rather than trusting ourselves to know the difference between fact and fiction, and continuing to try to ferret out the proof of infidelity will cause deep damage to our relationships. Maybe we can see a pattern where we've chosen someone who can't commit, or see a path of failed relationships because we couldn't trust even when our significant other hadn't done anything unfaithful. Maybe we've been choosing partners that couldn't be faithful (for their own reasons).

Understand that our actions based on suspicion aren't logical at all. They are driven by emotions such as fear, insecurity, anger and frustration. If someone strays, it's not about us! It's about his or her own insecurities, fears, and lack of self-worth. It's not a reflection on us. I know this because 80% of those I've worked with who are struggling with jealousy feel that somehow it is their fault, and that if they were more lovable, attractive, or attentive, then their partner would not have strayed or wouldn't think of straying.

So central in all of this is our own self-esteem, which translates to trusting ourselves. Self-esteem is the root of the issue. It's our emotional minds that protect the belief that we're not good enough, and we formed that belief when we didn't have the facts. Trust is the glue that keeps a relationship together, but it begins with trusting ourselves! Without trust, everything crumbles. The fact is that whatever happened to compromise our self-esteem, our ability to trust what felt right, whether it was caused by an emotionally unavailable parent or a betraying boyfriend or girlfriend, did not make us unlovable. It did not make us at fault. It did not lessen us, or make us stupid or incapable.

Take time to examine the context of what you learned from your family regarding sex and relationships, on how to be a woman or man, on how to be a partner, and you may find that you misunderstood the context of what you learned, or that what you were told was just false. We can't change the content, because we learned what we learned, but we can change the context, the way we look at it. We can decide what the truth is for us, and make the shift to the belief that we are lovable, and to do that, we need to love ourselves first. I've often said to clients that what they believe becomes part of the fabric of their lives. If our lives are loveless, it is because we don't love ourselves. When we change the way we look at things, the things we look at change.

Sexual and romantic intimacy is important in relationships. It's not everything, but it's important nonetheless. We all need to belong, to feel love and to love, to enjoy physical contact. If we feel insecure or jealous, we need to challenge the feelings that drive our need to act like private investigators in our love relationship, and seek out help to re-frame our own relationships with ourselves! Loving ourselves will open us up to receiving healthy love in all areas of our lives.

Getting to know and understanding our patterns is a healthy way to stop self-sabotaging our intimate relationships. My pattern was to expect to be taken care of. It had been drilled into my head since childhood that a woman was nothing without a husband, but he had to be one that could support me and my children. Sex wasn't talked about directly, but the gossip between my mother and her friends about so-and-so's daughter acting like a tramp taught me plenty. Virginity was to be protected at all costs until marriage.

It took me years to finally see the pattern in my broken relationships. I needed to be supported, and the way I saw the men in my life was measured against how well he could make me happy. It never worked out in the long run because no man could be all things I expected. The perfect man really didn't exist. When I finally got up off the floor after the devastation of this realization, I began to re-write my beliefs about what was healthy for me in love and I stopped finger-pointing. I began to take 100% ownership of myself and what I brought to my relationships.

Why not challenge that inner critic by questioning if all the blame truly belongs on the other person for the demise of our relationships? We can make connections between what triggered us to lash out or run or stay when it wasn't good for us in a relationship. Who taught us this way of behaving? Who did that ex remind us of when we felt abandoned, attacked, or smothered?

Simply making the mental leap from what we think we know (I left because he didn't listen to me or she left because I couldn't give her the life she wanted) to how it's really connected to what we learned as children is a huge step in moving forward. Facing our past is an important part of this process. I learned to run from manipulating and controlling relationships. What I didn't know then, but now know through self-discovery, is that I chose self-righteous manipulators for my relationships who were really a reminder of my parents. It's what I knew, because I was controlled all through my childhood and teen years. I responded in adulthood like a child who has to run from judgment and who has no control. This was my legacy. Once we familiarize ourselves with our habitual defenses and responses, we can move from self-sabotaging behaviors to empowering behaviors and live a more liberated life in which we are more powerful and much more in control of our destiny.

- What are your self-sabotaging thoughts and behaviors in love relationships?

- Do you ever feel as if something always gets in the way of experiencing real fulfillment and happiness in your love relationships?

- Do you doubt your ability to attract a healthy relationship? (If so, list the reasons, because they're the indicators that you lack self-trust.)

- Do you distract yourself with other areas of your life in order to avoid your loneliness?

- What pattern(s) do you see taking place?

Notes:

"Food isn't Therapy"
~Author unknown

"To all the girls that think you're fat because you're not a size zero, you're the beautiful one, its society who's ugly."
~Marilyn Monroe

CHAPTER 14

Self-sabotage and weight

It's not all about what we eat! When we think about how to shed extra weight, what are the first things we think of? Eating better and exercising, right?

I know that's what most people think of, but as a Clinical Hypnotherapist and Mind Coach, I have found that focusing on diet and exercise first when trying to release weight isn't always the best approach.

Please understand me. It's not that diet and exercise aren't important, they are. Both diet and exercise help in maintaining a healthy body, but if the desire to eat well and exercise is not congruent at the subconscious level to feeling that we are safe doing so, then we're just setting ourselves up for failure. If the subconscious believes that weight keeps any perceived danger away, it will be far more resourceful at keeping it on than our conscious willpower will ever be to keep that commitment to lose weight. As we know by now, our subconscious mind is 95% more powerful and efficient, and wins every time. We might lose the weight temporarily, but over time, the weight slowly creeps back and we lose our faith that we'll ever achieve our goals despite trying every known diet and weight-loss technique known to man.

The issue of weight has become one of my passions. It's is one of the most challenging subjects, due to the nature of the issue itself. It's also one of the most rewarding when I can help my clients understand what's happening to them.

As a society, we are obsessed with being thin, because the media bombards us with gazillions of ads about being beautiful. It saddens me when I'm out and hear comments made about someone who is overweight. It happened at a coffee shop a while ago when I was standing in line next to a table occupied by two ladies. I heard one whisper to the other that the couple a few tables over should stop 'stuffing their faces'. I looked, and noticed that the couple was indeed overweight. Now, I understand that this was her belief and that she wasn't really trying to be malicious, but I called this stranger on her comment and made the decision to share my belief that her judgment was hurtful, even if the couple didn't hear her. I wasn't popular and my opinion wasn't met with smiles. It's not that I'm perfect, or Mother Teresa. It's that I tend to ask myself what happened to these people to make them form a shield of weight around their own bodies to protect themselves. I ask what happened when I see homeless people, or those that seem down on their luck. I guess my work has taught me to look well below what I see on the surface to understand human nature.

The problem with weight, whether it's fifteen, thirty, or one hundred pounds, is not all about what we eat but about the emotion or emotions that have been attached to food and / or the act of consuming food. It's about how eating makes us feel. We may eat because food 'feeds' the emotion and fills that 'empty' feeling, whether we're hungry or not. In my practice, I've found that people feel that empty feeling in their stomach when we are investigating where the feeling being fed is located.

Case in point. Have you ever had a crappy day, and then fought traffic to get home? Once you're out of your work clothes and into comfy yoga pants, have you headed for a snack that involves chocolate or something salty? Or have you been bored and gone on a hunt through the fridge or all your cupboards looking for that something that will fill the emptiness? Have you taken down a bag of cookies and sat in front of the TV and suddenly realized the bag is empty? (No, little red ninja gremlins did not steal your cookies.) You ate them in a hypnotic trance! You may have sat down after a satisfying dinner and within a short time felt as if you needed something more.

There are a plethora of emotional reasons for reaching for food that have nothing to do with hunger. Boredom, frustration, anxiety, worry, sadness, and anger are a few. Happiness can also prompt us to eat, so it's not all about the negative feelings.

We can't just stop eating. Obviously not, we need food for fuel. Can we eat less? Absolutely, but beware of trying to starve the body. It will respond by dropping weight but over time, it will put it back on, because it's the program playing that directs the body. It's also a fact that diets don't work because they trigger a feeling of deprivation, a primal state that causes people to hoard, collect, or crave more of something, including food.

I know because I've felt it. It's like the pink elephant in the room. The more we tell ourselves not to think about it, the bigger and bigger it becomes till it's crushing us. Habit is only a small part of the weight issue; the biggest part is the emotional part, the 'why' of why we eat. The eating habit came after the feeling was poked and prodded by our lives. What needs to be done is to locate and eliminate the emotional triggers to eating. When we coma eat, or secretly eat (I've had clients that hide food so that they can snack away when no-one is around to avoid the guilt. Sad note: they still felt guilty), or lie to ourselves to justify the heaped plate of food or the pile of dainty tarts, we are acting according to the plan and it's very efficient.

What's driving the eating habit? You guessed it, win the prize… the subconscious mind. This part of the mind knows exactly why we eat, because it formed the habit of eating as a response to filling a emotional void. It's trying to sooth the hurts, the anxiety, the fears, and the stress to make us feel better, even if only temporarily. It simulates the feeling of love with the sensation of fullness and warmth. For some, it's a reward for all the things they feel they lack in their lives. Many former clients found that their emotional eating was in the evening, when they were bored, lonely or frustrated.

Consider again that the conscious / rational mind is only 5% of the brain. The other 95% is the subconscious. Which do you think will win over the battle with weight? Yup…the powerful subconscious mind.

The subconscious mind holds every emotional memory we've ever experienced, and if weight management is an issue, there are a number of 'emotional' memories that started the process, all the way back to childhood. Through the years, these emotional memories were triggered by situations relating to not just our weight, but to our physical appearance. Over time, they strengthened the mind's need to build a shield around us, and the more we believe in something (i.e. that we can't lose weight) the more it happens. The more we encounter situations that strengthen that belief, the stronger and more ingrained it becomes.

Here are some examples I've recorded from client childhood experiences about their associations with food equaling comfort:

- The only time there was harmony, or the illusion of harmony, in the family was meal-time together (that was my house).

- Mom showed her love through her cooking and baking.

- When you were upset, someone, like Gramma, or Mom, or Auntie, offered you cookies or ice cream to 'make you feel better'.

- When you were at a childhood friend's house, there was always a snack, and you felt good being taken care of, and sharing with, your friend.

- Eating between meals wasn't allowed as a household rule, so you learned to sneak food and treats. Food became that 'risky' high.

Today, we are all conscious of the ingredients and the sugar / fat content in our boxed food or in our recipes when we prepare a meal. We know that there are 350 calories and xxx fat grams per serving of pie or cake or (fill in the blank). Yet we eat it anyway.

Why? Because the following rationalizations act as the force used to bring the food to our mouths:

- If I can lose weight, I'll just gain it all back anyway
- I suck at dieting. Why bother trying?
- I'll be overweight no matter what I do
- I feel less 'empty' because when I eat the cake, it makes me feel better
- I'll eat better tomorrow

Here, too, are some subconscious reasons for emotional eating, which were birthed from the thoughts attached to the childhood 'good feeling' we got from eating when we learned the world was a confusing place:

- When you're thin, your partner wants more intimacy and you struggle with feeling close to him.
- Extra weight makes you less attractive so you'll get less attention from the opposite sex which keeps you from ultimately being rejected or abandoned.
- If you're thin, you will leave your relationship and be 'bad'.
- If you're thin, there will more expectations of you by others to be a success. If you're overweight, you'll deemed lazy so no one expects too much of you.

Remember, these are subconscious beliefs around our perception of self, formed before we had time to know if they were true or not.

Knowledge is power, and knowing ourselves is the only way to change. When we're digging through cupboards or heading for the fridge, we can try stopping a moment and listening for the subconscious cause of our eating. We can question what we're feeling that has us acting like a zombie or a heat-seeking missile. It's not all about the food we eat or the portion size (although it's important to develop and maintain healthy food selections and portions). Our conscious mind doesn't know what the true drive behind our inability to keep weight off is. It can't remember the first time we used food to soothe an emotional state, nor does it recall our feelings. At best, the conscious mind relies on willpower and factual knowledge on dieting to lose weight or try harder the next time we go on a diet. Watch how quickly willpower disappears. All that knowledge about caloric intake, the newest diet, the diet pills that will 'change your metabolism" is drawn on rationally to attempt to change an emotional habit. We draw on our conscious mind, even though it can't change how we feel on a deeper level. Change can only be affected at the subconscious mind level, so only changes there will lead to changing our habits.

When we struggle and go from diet to diet, we're likely to continue the trend unless we get to the emotional reason(s). Now, I realize that some of us have kept the weight at bay for years. Did we somehow compensate? If we did, was it in a healthy way? People who lose and gain weight end up believing it's their fault they can't keep it off, and when the weight comes back, they feel shame, guilt, and failure, which brings down self-esteem. People will do just about anything to keep the weight off, even if their dieting is a bad habit disguised as a good one. Just because being slender looks healthy, doesn't mean it is. Even working out six days a week is compensating. Don't get me wrong, fitness is good, but when it becomes a fixation it can become an addiction. Is that a better option? Logically it seems so. Some people restrict their diets and are rigid in deeming certain foods 'bad'. Would it not be better to add a little give in a healthier food and exercise plan?

What I'm trying to say is that without looking at the source of what caused us to lose self-esteem in the first place, and what drove the body to hold onto excess weight as a way to block out the pain of being hurt, rejected, and disappointed, the subconscious mind will find another way to fulfill the need to protect our original belief. Only by changing the program at the subconscious root level will habits and belief systems change. This will resonate with many, because we begin to realize it was solely about what we ate, or how often, or at what time of the day. It was about the emotions that were being fulfilled with food. This is how the subconscious protects us from feeling the stuff we don't like!

For example, look at why we eat when we feel sad. It falsely gives us the sense of being full, which is a metaphor for happy. We may not even notice that this is the reason why we reach for something to put in our mouths. If we observed ourselves a bit further, we would notice that the feeling we're feeding is in our stomach. Sadness often feels like emptiness. For some of my clients, the feeling was frustration about a life event and food was a way the subconscious mind found to soothe that frustration. The subconscious mind's job is to find a process to quell a feeling.

What would happen if we dealt with the feeling, even if just in the moment, with an associated thought pattern, like 'I'm sad at the thought of being alone' or 'I'm afraid to fail'? If, instead of eating when we don't need the fuel, we call a friend to meet for coffee, or we write out our frustrations in a journal, or we beat a pillow to release anger (don't knock it until you try it. It works!) or if we even have a good cry, then the need to eat for comfort would dissipate, and the body, which follows the mind, would release the weight over time. The change must happen in the mind before the body, because it's the mind that activates the body to do its bidding. By bringing our conscious awareness to the emotions that are fueling our habits, we are a step up the ladder towards lightness.

Notes:

> "Money has never made man happy, nor will it, there is nothing in its nature to produce happiness. The more of it one has the more one wants."
> ~**Benjamin Franklin**

CHAPTER 15

Self-sabotage and money

How do you feel about money? Is it your friend or foe? Does it slip through your fingers when you have it, like fine sand? Do you enjoy it, but save up for the future, or do you hoard it like a kid who doesn't want to share?

Some people live for the excitement of purchasing something new. We buy some "bling", a new gadget, or several new pairs of shoes. It breaks the boredom of our lives. It becomes a reward, a distraction from the routine of our lives, and that can lead to going into debt, which takes the shine off our love of shoes. Some people buckle down and work hard to pay down debt, trying to control their habit, but to use spending as a way to reward ourselves and to feel better about our lives is an addiction, and it strengthens with every new thing we purchase. The buzz of the feeling will fizzle out like day-old Coke. I've had clients that even became addicted to the challenge of accumulating debt and paying it down. It made them feel capable and in control. The problem is, if we can't break our addiction to financial excitement, we'll never have a healthy relationship with money, and we'll find ourselves a yo-yo to our need to 'spend'.

What we believe about money defines our relationship with it. If that belief is one that has us putting our urges for things above our means of buying them, then we're on the road called self-sabotage. I have coined the nickname the 'Poverty Syndrome'. I've lived with it most of my life. Think about it. Growing up, our parents' views about money influenced our own belief. Did we grow up hearing, 'money doesn't grow on trees', or 'we don't have extra for that toy'? Maybe we heard a conversation between adults that gave us the impression money was bad, such as 'Tom bought a fancy new car. He can't really afford it by the looks of his house. He thinks he's better than everyone else'.

I never lacked for the essentials, but I grew up hearing a lot of complaining that there was never enough money. That we paid cash for purchases so if we didn't have the cash, no buying. We stayed with our job until retirement to get the pension and to have job security. Sure, that was many years ago, but it influenced how I view money. At ten years old, I took my first summer job babysitting our neighbor's kids, because I wanted a K-Tel record and my Mom said that I'd have to wait till Christmas. What I heard was that here wasn't enough money for what I wanted so I wasn't important. Part-time jobs became my independence, and although I made money over my teen years, I made sure to save for the rainy day, because that's what I learned from my family - and it was a generational theme, going way back.

As human beings, we want to feel good all the time, and that's not possible. Any external factor can throw the switch from happy, to angry, or sad, or anxious in a nanosecond. Because we want to avoid those negative feelings, we find habits to distract us and keep them away. It's no different than someone addicted to smoking, drinking, or constantly working out at a gym. Yes, even a seemingly healthy activity, when taken to an extreme to feed an emotional need, is an addiction.

Take boredom. Boredom can be a strong motivator in seeking out ways to avoid feeling sad, or down, or alone. We may be sitting there in a den or living room at night in front of our laptops and find our fingers typing in Ebay.com or theshoppingchannel.com. Then we see a new car part, a killer dress, or those 'I have to have them' awesome pair of shoes. Next thing you know you've bought it! It's easy when we aren't physically handing over the cash - it's just a transaction that happens in the virtual world. It can be like hypnotic driving, only it's hypnotic buying, and we're not thinking about our credit card limit. We're subconsciously avoiding the feeling that defines boredom, which is sadness. We may be sad at the thought of being alone, sad at the thought of not feeling connected to others, sad at the thought of not having friends, or sad at the thought of feeling sad.

We subconsciously looked for, and found, something that avoids the sad, but it's like filling our fuel tank with windshield wiper fluid - it's not what's needed. A fleeting reward may leave us feeling better for a minute, an hour, or a day, but eventually it goes away, because like negative feelings, good feelings can't last 24/7.

In Freudian psychoanalysis, there is a term called the Pleasure Principle. It's the subconscious seeking of pleasure to avoid pain in order to satisfy the needs of our body and mind. The subconscious mind wants whatever feels good at the time, with no consideration for the reality (logical mind) of the situation. The need overrides the logical consequences, such as going into debt and not being able to pay the rent or mortgage because of over-spending. Our subconscious mind is goal-oriented to feed our needs, so it locks onto those behaviors that will satisfy the need, regardless of the consequences. When we fulfill needs responsibly, it's all good, and it feels good, but we're not always responsible.

When we let the feelings associated with lack, such as boredom, or frustration, override our logic, then we can wreak havoc on our lives. It's easy to just slap down a credit card and worry about it later. It's fulfilling the need in the moment (self-sabotaging behavior) and ignoring the logical mind's input (don't buy that because the rent's due).

I truly believe that how we use money tells us so much about how we feel about ourselves. Do we use money to buy things for others to please them? Do we spend money on things we don't need and 'impulse buy'? Do we always feel there isn't enough money, even when we have a cushion put away in the bank (that was me)? Our beliefs that money is bad, or there isn't enough of it, are because we don't feel worthy of financial abundance. We don't feel worthy of having enough, or more than enough. We feel stuck in the mind-loop of 'not having enough'. We feel we're lacking inside, and to avoid the feelings associated with it, we may spend too much or hoard too much, never having a friendly relationship with money.

Something in our early years made us believe that having money, or conversely believing that we'll never have enough money, drives our behavior. We may think we deserve to be rich, but our beliefs aren't in alignment with that. Some of my clients who had gambling and shopping addictions said it was the only time they felt excited and alive, even knowing they were using up the credit they had, and they did it regardless of whether their spouses and families were going to be affected. It was 'pure in the moment' impulse, because they didn't feel good enough, or feel that they had anything 'exciting' to look forward to in their lives.

Money is good. Money becomes our friend when we learn to have a healthy relationship with it and to respect it. It does not buy love, nor does it fix our negative feelings long-term. Uncover what our critical inner voice is saying, and delve deeper to understand what the internal need really is that is erroneously being fed. Maybe we don't overspend and have a healthy bank account, but still feel that no matter how much we save there still isn't enough. The same principle applies.

How to help identify our relationship with money:

- Make a list of ways you have self-sabotaged yourself with money in the past and list what you can do now instead.

- Make a list of the thoughts you have associated with money and begin to look at how you came to have those beliefs.

- Do you have difficulty holding onto money because you subconsciously believe you don't deserve to be successful?

- If you hoard money, is it because you internally believe that you'll lose it to that bad event that is somewhere around the corner?

- Do you need to spend your money as soon as you have it, because you want the instant reward and believe that the money won't last anyway so you need to do it now?

We need to create a change in perception, and a handle on our relationship with money. Our thoughts about money are energy, and the longer we have the 'lack' mindset, the longer we'll be seeing money fly through our fingers or not land there at all. We can start by simply reframing what our negative belief with a positive spin. For example, rather than saying 'I never have enough money at the end of the month', say 'My bank balance is increasing everyday and I always have enough money for myself', or 'Money and I are friends and we support each other'. Yes, it sounds like the Law of Attraction idea, and it is. What we put out there, we receive. Just be consistent, and fake it until it feels good when you say it - remembering that the thought of money is energy, and you are energy, so why not attract each other?

Notes:

> *"When you are inspired by some great purpose, some extraordinary project, all your thoughts break their bonds: Your mind transcends limitations, your consciousness expands in every direction, and you find yourself in a new, great and wonderful world. Dormant forces, faculties and talents become alive, and you discover yourself to be a greater person by far than you ever dreamed yourself to be!"*
> **~Patanjali**

CHAPTER 16

Letting your 'Greater than you think you are' plan guide you

Letting your 'Greater than You Think You Are' plan guide you in life will lead you to inspiration and self-acceptance. Powerful advice, right? It works, as all the mindfulness authors agree, and lil'old me believes it does as well. Having your own self-care plan - a list of daily practices to foil your 'inner saboteur' will help you develop the healthy habits that will make you feel more energized, relaxed, and balanced.

That doesn't mean you can park your butt in the shade of a tree on a sunny day waiting for good fortune to fall from that cerulean blue sky and hit you on the head. There's action required on your part, and that involves feeling your 'feelings'. Get intimate with them. Emotions power your thoughts, and your intentions are attached to them like the basket is attached to the hot air balloon, but if your head is firmly planted in the sand or floating willy-nilly in the air, how will you know if you're being led to follow the plan that is bigger than your rational mind could ever compute?

Your part of the plan is to listen to your own innate and 'older than time' guidance system...your feelings. When an opportunity presents itself, whether from the outside world (someone tells you about a job opportunity just when you were contemplating leaving the one you're in; your client cancels an appointment so you have time to run out for lunch and 'happen' to run into an old friend who you reconnect with) or your inner world (suddenly feeling inspiration over a thought that is emerging in your mind), gauge the feeling for its rightness for you. Take the time to savor the sweetness of its texture on your tongue, the fullness if its weight in your stomach, the lightness of its energy in your chest. Be aware!

But - and there is a 'but' here - this isn't an overnight process. It takes time, and persistent + consistent + time = success. It's going to take small steps of doing small things everyday for yourself, such as being aware of your negative self-talk (observe); catching it, questioning it, and challenging it. That will begin the creation of a new thought pattern. Use what you wrote and observed from the chapters we've already covered. Do this consistently, and it becomes a habit, and creates positive patterns. It only takes twenty-one days of consistent thought and action to form a new habit. Make time to write / journal your feelings, or meditate (or both) for ten to fifteen minutes daily. It doesn't have to be for hours. Surround yourself with positive things; people, places, or things. I find inspiration in reading, so I do my best to read a chapter or two of a book that is uplifting and teaches me about bettering myself every day.

Keep following that course, even if it may look to you like a detour in the road, a sometimes crazy zig to your rational side's zag. Trust that you will zig just where you're meant to. All the twists, turns, road blocks, trip ups, stumbles, and straight lines are part of your journey on the road of your life.

What's your self-care plan?

Notes:

"And the day came when the risk to remain tight in a bud was more painful than the risk it took to blossom"
~Anais Nin

"What is more mortifying than to feel that you have missed the plum for want of courage to shake the tree?"
~Logan Pearsall

CHAPTER 17

A leap of faith with courage and strength

A leap of faith. Yes, it takes courage. Yes, it takes determination. Yes, it may be against what we feel inside. Yes, it may make us feel vulnerable - but what if the Universe has our backs – no matter what? How much braver would we be? How many more chances would we take at work and in our relationships?

When we are ready to take the conscious leap and make the connection that what you want wants you, then you can start moving towards what you want. And as I explained earlier, what you think and feel and what you are attracting with those thoughts and feelings are always in harmony. So if you don't like what you're drawing into your life, empower yourself to make changes.

As many of you may already be familiar with the Law of Attraction, you know that it's all about energy. And everything is energy.

The Universe responses to the vibration of our thoughts and the feeling attached to them related to the story we tell about our lives. And if we put out a sad, angry or 'less than' story, we attract those people and events that match up with the story.

If we've been contemplating it, then maybe we're ready. If we reach for courage, which we all inherently have, we have the ability to use our creative juices, and the world becomes our classroom. If we reach for fear, or allow it to ensnare us, we are then only a participant in our lives, living in our own self-imposed prison.

Life is about choices. And there are always many roads presented in life. The only thing you have power over is the decisions that you make, and how you will **act and react** to different situations.

So take the leap, people! There is nothing to lose if we're holding on to fear by our teeth. To reach our goals, we have to heal the fear that holds us back from what we want in life. It's courage that conquers fear. We'll always have challenges in life and fear hold us back from learning about who we are and what we can achieve in life.

I've always collected quotes that help me to see the good and aspire for something better for myself. The one at the top of the page is by Anais Nin, and the others which I quoted in earlier chapters are my favorites, and I use them in my work to illustrate concepts all the time. So here are a few to help you as you stand at the edge of the cliff looking out towards what you desire. The leap may seem daunting, but if you want what is making your heart sing to come true, then take the risk and leap!

"Don't fear failure so much that you refuse to try new things. The saddest summary of life contains three descriptions: could have, might have, and should have."
~**Louise E. Boone**

"Life shrinks or expands in proportion to one's courage"
~**Anais Nin**

"Those who wish to sing will always find a song."
~**Celtic Proverb**

"Why do you stay in prison when the door is so wide open?"
~**Rumi**

"Energy and persistence conquer all things."
~**Benjamin Franklin**

"Transformation is something I cannot explain - too much analysis might destroy it."
~**Sophia Loren**

"Fear less, hope more, eat less, chew more, whine less, breathe more, talk less, say more, hate less, love more, and good things will be yours."
~**Swedish Proverb**

"Don't ask yourself what the world needs; ask yourself what makes you come alive. And then go and do that. Because what the world needs is people who have come alive."
~**Harold Whitman**

"Be at least as interested in what goes on inside you as what happens outside. If you get the inside right, the outside will fall into place."
~**Eckart Tolle**

"Be not afraid of growing slowly. Be only afraid of standing still."
~**Chinese Proverb**

"Those who dance are called insane by those who don't hear the music."
~Eddie Vedder

"If you change the way you look at things, the things you look at change."
~Wayne Dyer

"I've missed more than 9000 shots in my career. I've lost almost 300 games. 26 times, I've been trusted to take the game winning shot and missed. I've failed over and over and over again in my life. And that is why I succeed."
~Michael Jordan

Notes:

> "When a defining moment comes along,
> you can do one of two things.
> Define the moment, or let the moment define you."
> **~Quote from the Movie 'Tin Cup'**

> "Life is like a game of cards. The hand that is dealt you represents determinism; the way you play it is free will."
> **~Jawaharal Nehru**

CHAPTER 18

Defining your moment

Webster's Dictionary defines free will as (1) voluntary choice or decision - *I do this of my own free will.* (2) freedom of humans to make choices that are not determined by prior causes

The second definition resounds with a lot of truth for me. By tapping into our free will, we can make a choice that is not about our past experiences, our failures, or our fears of the unknown. It lets us make a choice based on what feels right in the moment. It can be as simple as going on a date after a very long hiatus, and ignoring the self-talk that tells us it will probably not go well, and that he'll be a misogynistic ass like the last dozen. It can be as complicated as having anxiety in the days leading up to quitting day at work and beginning to doubt the decision, but going through with it anyway because the job is toxic. These are all real examples from clients I've worked with. Every person is the true source of his or her thoughts and actions.

Within every moment is the beauty of free will. No-one holds a gun to our heads to make us do anything. Even someone's cruel words towards us have no effect when we know who we are. There again is free will - the choice to choose to act on what is said or done to us, or to ignore it so that their words fall off us like water off a duck's back.

If we listen to our gut, if we open ourselves to our intuition, we will make the right decision in the moment. Each of us has an instinctual barometer which alerts us to the right road to take on given journey. How many times have we done something based on what our head told us, and not our heart or gut - and how many times have we later told ourselves 'I should have listened to my gut' because our head led us in the wrong direction? I know I have.

We must try not to rush when making choices, though, no matter how important they may be. It's in the quiet space between the musical notes that we find the meaning and emotional beauty of the piece. Without that quiet, it would all be noise. We need to silence ourselves to hear our inner voice among the chatter of the world. We'll hear it. As Ralph Waldo Emerson said 'Nothing can bring you peace but yourself. ' So listen!

We can learn to mediate, or even easier, just stop, close our eyes, and go inside ourselves. It's that simple, and in that silence, we must do our best to surrender. We can allow ourselves to compare our choices. The one that echoes back to us with joy, fullness, relief, warmth, happiness, or calmness is the one to go with, regardless of what our head is saying. It's the choice our heart and soul knows is right for us, and that feeling will come in the moment, not as an echo of the past. It's such a simple technique, yet so powerful.

Take time to be ready! We need to take the time to be the person we want to become and to have the life we want - we have to decide we're ready to show up! Be ready to shine with all our foibles and imperfections, and lay our fear of being ourselves to rest. If people can't, or won't, accept us for who we are, then we need to let them go. The most valuable and important person in our lives is not our partner, our child, or our boss...it's ourselves!

We can share our real selves, without excuses or explanations, with others. We all need our human connections. In fact, we're programmed to 'belong', and really suffer when our social bonds aren't present or we shy from making them, so get out there! We all need to be our savvy and remarkable selves!

We have to commit to showing up, every single day. Yes, I know some days are harder than others. There are days when I feel as if nothing I do matters, or that I'll never get what I so desire. We can have that pity party for a short while and then get over ourselves, and we can make small steps daily, whether it's getting out another resume, taking a dance class, or going out to audition for a choir. We just need to take that step into our lives!

We must be ready to roll with the highs and lows, and just keep plugging away. There will never be only highs or only lows. That gives us hope. The highs and lows give our life texture. They are the experiences that give us contrast, and allow us to make the choices to either fully occupy our space or shrink away within it. No-one will give us a free bucket of love, self-respect, or self-esteem.

If we're aware that life won't always be effortless, or glamorous, or a cake-walk, we can acknowledge that it can be ugly, awkward, inelegant, boring, and painful. So when it is, do we quit? Do we bury ourselves under the covers and wish it all away? No! We take the pain and make it work for us, let it push us to grow. There's a saying I like that can whip me back on track: 'Never grow a wishbone where your backbone ought to be'. Start planting that backbone seed!

Then (drum roll) act! Even if it's small move towards something better, we've defined the moment by making a choice that feels right to us and for us. Understand that we are amazing beings! We are powerful, we are talented, and we are uniquely ourselves! Whether we wake to a sunny day or a gray, rainy day, we are always whole, skilled, capable, and worthy people. We must embrace our greatness, because it's there, no matter what that critical inner voice says. We can stop beating ourselves up and starting loving ourselves again.

OK...I've been getting all worked up here to inspire you and now I need a nap!

Notes:

> "What a liberation to realize that the 'voice in my head' is not who I am. 'Who am I, then?' The one who sees that."
> ~**Eckhart Tolle**

> "Smile, breathe, and go slowly"
> ~**Thich Nhat Hanh**

CHAPTER 19

Give up your story

Freedom comes when we finally choose to let go and give up our stories. When we let go of all that we think we are and move towards what and who we really are, we become limitless. It's like discovering wings and deciding, while standing on the edge of the nest, to leap out.

If we listen closely to ourselves, whether or not we've reached the depths of despair, there will come a moment when we will find that it's necessary to let things go. Misery can be a huge motivator! At our lowest point, we may finally decide that living 'less than' isn't an option anymore, that we've had enough, and that we just can't carry that 800 pound gorilla on our backs!

Friends of mine, a mother and her daughter, lost a loved one recently, and I realized that we're at the age when we start to lose the ones we love who are older than we are. It could be a mother; it could be a sister, a brother, or a father. It could be a dear friend or a pet. Maybe you've already experienced this type of loss. I'm fortunate that I still have both parents in good health, but losing the ones we love comes with the territory. This reminded me how important it is to live my life, and to live it as big as I can. None of us knows how much time we have on this earth, and it's important to relish the essence of every day, as best we can.

It reminded me that we must keep listening to that often-silenced voice within us for the truth of who we are...infinite, boundless, loving, and always whole. We know that our time on this Earth is not just time to struggle or to fight, least of all ourselves. We need to let that go. This time that we have here is to return to love, to the very essence of who we are. Instead of worrying about the past or the future so much, we must stay present and appreciate what we're still able to do with our circumstances.

Life is a like a dance between doing and not doing, between wanting and patience, between moving forward and surrender. It's a movement of living our purpose and allowing our purpose to live with us and for us. Sometimes the rhythm is slow, and sometimes it's fast, but we can keep up - just flow with it and keep dancing.

We can all let go of limiting beliefs that hold us back, upend that heavy knapsack that's bending us backwards in a way we're not meant to bend. There are many good reasons to do it. Maybe it's because those crappy beliefs are just too heavy (think of a gorilla on our back). Maybe it's because they are shackling us. Maybe it's because we are constantly tripping over them like a piece of uneven pavement, leaving us with bleeding knees. Maybe it's because we're tired of the pain of those bloodied knees!

Consider that our stories weren't entirely written by us - not even close. Each chapter from the very first was filled with all the should-haves and could-haves and don'ts spoken by many voices that weren't ours at all! We may have forgotten that, or never even realized that we learned to look to the world to define us, and nothing's really changed since - we still do. We do it when we worry about how we'll be perceived, or when we question what we want for ourselves.

Pick up the pen and begin again with the ink of free will. We can choose not to wear our story like an old pair of pants that are torn, or just too tight to get into anymore. Visualize lying on the bed, trying to zip up those cool jeans that are two sizes too small. You might eventually get them zipped but once you're standing, you can't breathe or the top button flies off like a high speed bullet. We can choose instead to courageously go through our 'closet' and throw out what no longer suits us nor fits our tastes, including those torturous jeans. Let the story we re-write breathe. Give it room to bend to the winds of change and the flexibility to allow for choices as we desire them.

We can let go of anger and fear that block our ability to speak our truth. We can let go of the sadness that prevents love from flowing into or out of our hearts, and let go of the loneliness that may impede the friendship with ourselves from growing. How much more room would we have, with that space we create for the good things we deserve?

When we finally decide to give it all up, to do the work to grow and evolve, like a phoenix rising out of its own ashes, we ascend reborn, completely liberated, refreshed, and free. Within the newness are only those past beliefs that were good and healthy.

We can let go of the story that belonged to our family, to others' experiences that were placed in our knapsacks and choose to create our own. The best day of our life is the one on which we decide our life is our own, with no apologies or excuses, no-one to rely on or to blame. The gift is ours! It's an amazing journey and we alone are responsible for its quality.

This is the day our life really begins.

What parts of your story will you keep?

Which parts of your story will you replace?

Notes:

> "Trust yourself. Create the kind of self that you will be happy to live with all your life."
> ~**Golda Meir**

> "Nothing can bring you peace but yourself."
> ~**Ralph Waldo Emerson**

CHAPTER 20

Open up to trust!

Each day I'm blessed to partner with people who have decided that they've had enough of their self-sabotaging fears, insecurities, 'screw-ups', sadnesses, shames, angers, and guilts. I cannot tell you how empowering it feels to help them along on their journey, not from an ego state (aren't I great) but from the heart state (aren't I lucky).

I thank each and every client who I've had the opportunity to listen to, guide, cajole, empathize with, and educate, for honoring me with their memories of fear; who gave me their trust so that they could, in turn, heal through recapturing the trust within themselves. Each of them has given me the gift of learning, so that I have grown with each experience on this journey we call life.

My biggest lesson in this life has been to trust. Yes, self-trust. I would only let people in to a certain extent, even though I was perceived as open and engaging. I created a shield around my heart, because inside that secret place, I was afraid to be hurt and disappointed. I protected myself from feeling the sadness of my childhood perception that I was unlovable. 'Marshmallow on the outside and granite on the inside' is how I was once described by my wonderful husband. When he gave me this bit of wisdom, rather than getting angry at the perceived criticism (which had been my way of defending myself), I felt the truth of his statement, and doing so allowed me to ferret out more of the root cause of my distrust. I came to self-discovery through writing, observation, practice, and lots of hypnotherapy that led to clarity, with buckets of sweat, pain, and tears on the way to my enlightenment.

Am I there yet, at the top of the self-actualized mountain, pumping my fist in the air? Oh no, not I - because that's not how real life works. If I were at the apex of my growth, what would there be to look forward to? It's through the hurt of evolving that I grow, and in the aftermath, the soreness left in my body and mind tell me I've done something, that I've lived and can thrive versus just survive.

There are several ways that we can begin to find the observer side of ourselves, and begin to question that voice in our head that isn't that kind:

- Breathe. Just spending a few minutes each day breathing deeply can help clear the way for healing. Make sure you're somewhere comfortable and safe while doing this as at first you may get a little light-headed.

- Learn self-hypnosis (same idea as meditation): If you already self-hypnotize, explore adding a few extra minutes to deepen your practice. You never know where it may lead you! If you haven't added self-hypnosis to your toolkit, look at your local community centers or adult education options and find a course.

- Journal: Moving your negative feelings and emotions out of your body is a powerful way to get clarity and physical healing. Do your best (and it's more than good enough) to do a bit of journaling a few times a week - or daily if it suits you. Make it a part of you and not a chore.

I liken this process of becoming more aware of ourselves to waking from a dream. In the dream, we are being led by our subconscious mind as it processes what we experience externally. It leads us, based on our beliefs, through every waking moment, because the subconscious mind never sleeps. We have no control over what we dream about (unless we lucid dream, which is a dream in which we know we are dreaming). As our awareness grows through self-work, we find ourselves more conscious of our thoughts, their internal triggers, and the ensuing self-sabotaging habits. This is when we take back control. It's the opportunity to create something different. It can even happen when we're hurt, in pain, or licking the bottom of the barrel, and the voice of our inner guide gently asks, 'Have you had enough yet'? When the answer is yes, we begin walking the path to finding our authentic selves.

Through my work on my 'self' and through working with others, I have learned to deeply appreciate the value of trust. Trust is something we can't get from any one or any thing until we have it within ourselves to experience and apply to our world. I love the expression 'Your outer world is an expression of your inner world'. That means that if our world looks scary, or makes us angry, sad or lost, it's actually us using our feelings and perceptions to paint a dark sweep over our view of every situation we encounter.

I find myself being more and more authentic as my fear of letting people see the 'inner me' becomes lessened because I no longer judge myself so harshly. Am I perfect? Hell no. Am I done? Thankfully not. We are all works in progress, but each shift I make in my perception of myself - each old, false, ugly belief I overcome - brings me deeper into a state of peace. The more I observe how I feel, and the thoughts attached to those feelings, the more I am able to do the work to change and have more time in peacefulness.

> "Come to the edge.
> We might fall.
> Come to the edge.
> It's too high!
> COME TO THE EDGE!
> And they came, and we pushed,
> And they flew."
> **~Christopher Logue**

Notes:

> "May I be the wishing jewel, the vase of plenty,
> A word of power and supreme healing;
> May I be the tree of miracles."
>
> ~*Shantideva*

CHAPTER 21

Questions to ask yourself about all the good stuff that exists inside you

For many of us, it appears that being nasty to ourselves (putting ourselves down and mentally abusing our bodies) comes far more naturally than loving ourselves. If you've punished your own psyche for far too long, do your best to keep silencing your inner critic. If you don't, you're just perpetuating despair.

It makes me cringe when I think of all the nasty, hateful ways I programmed myself, by saying the same horrible things over and over again. I can't tell you how many hours I've spent caught in mental self-flagellation and inner fighting caused by my ego trying to justify my sense of lack.

It sometimes feels too hard to practice self-compassion. Compassion towards others has always been a cornerstone of my being, but compassion towards myself - that's a heck of a lot harder. It's a battle I choose to no longer participate in. I <u>have</u> to choose, over and over again, to walk away from my inner fighting when I back-slip. I try to remind myself to stop and ask myself some no-nonsense questions to help me observe whether I'm moving towards shifting my beliefs about myself or if I'm stuck in the loop. I hope they help you move towards a healthier way interacting with yourself as well.

1. Are you self-compassionate?

I just read about research being done on the human condition, and how it relates to how we view ourselves, including a 2007 study by Berkeley's Juliana Breines and Serena Chen that suggests that *self-compassion*, rather than self-esteem, may be the key to unlocking our true potential for greatness. Maybe that's semantics, but I don't think so. Maybe I've had it wrong (and my 'compassionate self' forgives me, because it's OK to question and I'm human), or maybe they're two sides of a coin. (I like that idea!)

Self-esteem is 'confidence in one's own worth or abilities; self-respect'. Self-compassion, by contrast, is defined as 'extending compassion to one's self in instances of perceived inadequacy, failure, or general suffering'. Dr. Kristin Neff, a pioneering researcher on self-compassion, defines self-compassion as being composed of three main components - self-kindness, common humanity, and mindfulness.

Self-compassion is allowing yourself to look at yourself and everything that makes you 'you' - including all of your perceived mistakes and deficiencies - with empathy and consideration. It allows you to embrace the reality that to err is human. When you're self-compassionate in times when life gets hard, you neither judge yourself with boxing gloves, nor feel the need to defend yourself to yourself or to anyone else. Self-compassion leads to great levels of happiness, self-security, and self-trust.

2. Is what you're telling yourself the truth?

Ask yourself if your thoughts are really the truth. I find I have to step back and observe my thoughts, to determine whether they're actually true. Examples like 'I'm not smart enough', or 'I'll never be good enough' are things I've repeated to myself as a matter of course - and I've come to recognize that they're really false!. As Byron Katie astutely put it 'Don't believe everything you think.' I now do my best to constantly remind myself that my inner critic's opinion of me is often a load of crap, and I do myself the deepest disservice by believing what it says. Self-loathing is a product of wrong thinking.

Write down your thoughts on your most repeated nasty quotes. The more you know them, the more you can catch them.

3. What makes you utterly unique?

There's only one you! It's your responsibility to be yourself, and no-one else can or will ever step into that role. You're the only you who'll ever exist in the entire expanse of the universe, uniquely you, powerful and mighty. Pretty freaking amazing, right?

So what makes you 'you'? What makes you a unique, remarkable, a one-of-a-kind person? Think about it. Write it down. Laugh at your zaniness, your exceptional amazing traits, your distinctive way of looking at the world, with all your perceived quirks and eccentricities. You are here to bring those qualities into the world. Amen to that! Write down what makes you unique.

4. Whose expectations are you trying to meet?

I've often judged myself based on expectations that were passed down to me by my family, bosses, partners, friends, and even those based on societal norms. What I've been learning over the years is that they aren't my standards, they're someone else's, and as I've never been one to follow the rules at all times, I found myself rebelling many a time.

So why did I continue to try to live up to someone else's ideals? Why did I blindly follow a credo I don't support? Who said I'm supposed to be financially secure by a certain age? Why do I have to look a certain way, act a certain way, or speak a certain way? Assessing the foundation of my beliefs and reminding myself what I truly value allows me to be far less self-judgmental. Think about the expectations you have for yourself and others and try to identify where they came from in the first place.

5. Do you know how powerful your impact is on others?

Your words and your presence have an effect on those who are part of your life. When you tell someone they look great, or notice a new haircut, you spark good feelings in the other person. When you respond sarcastically, or with boredom, anger, or frustration, you also spark feelings in the other person, usually those of hurt.

If you have a driven desire to impact others, then do it. Don't stop yourself because you think you've got nothing to offer, or don't have what it takes to help inspire others or to make a difference in this world. Just remember to use compassion, to be non-judgmental, and to be kind and considerate when you step into the world to bring forth your greatness.

It doesn't have to be done with impressive displays or gestures. Even sharing your smile with another has an impact. We never know if our actions will help another grow or get up off the floor, but when we come from a place of peace, not ego, it'll make what you do rely less on outcomes or accolades.

Your simplest acts are powerful, because the recipient of your words and gestures may feel so good that they pay it forward. Don't underestimate or play down your own individual power.

Remember any acts, words or gestures from you that made someone (or many people) feel good and ask yourself - what made it uniquely you?

6. **Do you have any secret desires on ways to bring your exclusive 'you-ness' to your family, your community, your workplace, or to the world?**

Your subconscious mind makes up 95% of the power of your mind; the conscious mind only 5%. The subconscious mind protects what you believe about yourself, good and bad, without judging it or analyzing if those beliefs are positive or negative. The subconscious acts on what you stored, and it forgets nothing. It believes what you believe about your worth and place in this world. The subconscious is the feeling mind, and so it doesn't think. The conscious mind is the thinker, and it rationalizes based on skills learned, by comparing options, and it looks for logic in life to keep us sane.

If you think you want to change, and use logical willpower to do it, you will fail against the power of the subconscious mind, because until the subconscious feels that you believe something different, you will not change regardless of how much you think you can.

This is why to stop self-sabotage, you have to find the subconscious belief that is working against you. It's always based on not feeling good enough. By bringing your negative self-talk, habits, and behavior to your awareness and challenging each of them, you are already taking the first step. By bringing positive self-talk, your good morals and values, and all your unique gifts to the forefront, you will enhance each step all the more. So keep going!

> *"Our negative thoughts are valuable messages to us about our deeper fears and negative attitudes. These usually are so basic to our thinking and feeling that we don't realize they are beliefs at all. We assume that they are simply "the way life is." We may be consciously affirming and visualizing prosperity, but if our unconscious belief is that we don't deserve it, then we won't create it. Once we become aware of our core negative beliefs, they begin to heal."*
> **~Shakti Gawain**

Notes:

> "Unless Commitment is made, there are only promises and hopes but no plans."
> **~Peter Drucker**

> "Be not afraid of greatness; some are born great, some achieve greatness, and others have greatness thrust upon them."
> **~William Shakespeare**

CHAPTER 22

Commitment

Commitment - the state or quality of being dedicated to a cause, activity, etc.

'Commitment' evokes a strong sense of intention and focus. There is no-one who deserves our respect, our commitment, or our vow of self-belief more than ourselves. If we can't make a commitment to ourselves that we will break our molds, clear the old beliefs out of our mental attic, polish our inner silver, then we devalue ourselves. We aren't 'showing up' in our lives.

I know we all learned as little kids that to make a promise was sacred, and breaking one was like a mortal sin - or justification for a good butt-slapping in my house growing up. A promise is a declaration, while a commitment is the action and intention to do something with dedication.

Be committed versus just declaring promises. Here are some commitments that I've brought into my life that have helped me move from feeling that I'm never going to be good enough to opening to the truth that I am always good enough. I encourage you to learn what these sentences mean to you. Commitment makes the whole thing more purposeful, but commitment without feeling is just a way to fool yourself. As I tell my clients, 'fake it until you make it'. The more you practice, the more the statements shift into truth. The feeling invoked by the statement is always the barometer as to whether the thought is true for you or not. At first, it might not feel true, but by committing to elevating yourself, by committing to opening up to what's so good inside you, you will come to the point where it is true and congruent with your thoughts and feelings.

So here's something you can add to your self-care plan: a list of practices to diminish your 'inner saboteur'. Do your best to commit to practicing one daily, or weekly, or monthly until it feels honest inside you. Once they do, these statements become beliefs and affirmations that can become part of your life for keeps. It's something you need to do a little at a time, because over time they are compounded and become your reality. You can tell yourself a lie long enough that you forget it's not true, which is what you've been doing, by the way. So take that same principle and tell yourself the truth until you believe it!

- I commit to seeing myself as a whole person and not one who is lacking.

- I commit to making peace with what I think I lack so that I can let it go.

- I commit to falling in love with myself a little more every day as I learn to appreciate my uniqueness.

- I commit to being kinder when I speak to myself of myself.

- I commit to challenging those thoughts and feelings that have continuously led me astray.

- I will write them down and then rip them up.

- I commit to appreciating myself more than I appreciate others for I deserve the appreciation.

- I commit to sharing a smile with others, whether I know them or not, because it costs me nothing to do so.

- I commit that I will do my best to live in the moment and see the blessings in my life.

- I commit to reaching out to those I trust when I am in need, because I'm worthy of loving care and attention.

- I commit to letting go of anger and control, because I only control myself and I choose peace.

- I commit to listening to my inner voice and to my heart when making decisions, rather than to what others think I need or should do.

- I commit to hugging myself daily because it's OK to need to be held.

- I commit to hugging my loved ones, even if it's out of my comfort zone and it freaks them out.

- I commit to laugh more, to live more and let fun waltz into my life.

- I commit to viewing my life as a gift unfolding with endless opportunity to connect with others, versus a solitary confinement cell in a cold prison.

- I commit to reminding myself how capable I am, rather than procrastinating and self-sabotaging.

- I commit not to allow anyone or anything to control me. My life is my own.

Notes:

> "Great satisfaction comes from sharing with others"
> ~*Unknown*

CHAPTER 23

Personal writings I'd like to share

Breath and Light
June, 2015

From breath and light I came to be,
to learn my worth, my destiny

No threatening hand nor sharpened tongue,
that I endured when I was young
Can blemish the glow I feel inside,
buried deep, compelled to hide
The story unfolded, as my life,
as Daughter, Sister, Mother and Wife

Beneath it all I longed to be
my Spirit; strong, bright and free!
My Mother's tongue cannot cut me down,
my Father's touch cannot make me drown
For the physical me is just a shell,
the part that did endure the hell
Of things a child should never see,
of expectations she could never be

Of moments, trapped and lost at sea,
Confused and hurt, was I them or me?

I look upon the lessons learned,
of all the things I wished and yearned
and through the dark I finally see,
that all that has shaped the who is me...
Forged of breath and light, to be,
I now hold my worth, my destiny
My choices are now free and clear,
to live my life, without the fear
A newborn babe cries at its birth.
As I am reborn, I claim my worth.
With joy in my voice and my heart,
I hold my space..it's a new start.

Living Whole
January, 2016

I hear myself breathing, one breath after another. Some breaths are gentle and rhythmic, others come shallow and tight. Either way, they show me I live. I must then be occupying space. Is this space mine? Is it mine to occupy fully? Must I question my right to "be" if in fact I live and breathe?

Does the rose climbing the trellis question its right to draw life-giving water and minerals from the soil it's rooted to? Does the smallest spider question its right to build a gossamer web wherever it chooses?

I, too, am. And by that one unquestionable reality I MUST assume my place in this Universe, with all that by right I am deserving of: Safety in mind and body; individuality; using my voice; to love and receive love without doubt or confusion; spiritual and intellectual growth; financial abundance.

My only limitation has been that I ever believed I was undeserving of abundance, unworthy, and lacking of that "certain something" that would make me feel whole. Yet I've always BEEN whole. Nothing is missing...just the truth hidden in the recesses of my mind under oily layers of lies. And this knowledge can work for me because the knowingness of the untruths expands me and shoots me forward out of the cannon of my desire. And I find my wings in flight...

I AM
2016

I am a Woman
I am a Woman who is a Mother
I am a Woman who is a Wife
I am a Woman who is a Daughter
I am a Woman who is a Sister
I am a Woman who is an Aunt
I am a Woman who is a Best Friend
I am a Woman who is a Professional
These are the tangibles

I am a Woman
I am a Woman who is passionate about
those things that move her
I am a Woman who is ready to fight for and defend what she believes in, no matter how much it may hurt or be ridiculed
I am a Woman who is proud of who she has become, knowing that her lessons have been both bitter and sweet on her tongue

Self-Sabotage: The Art of Screwing Up

> I am a Woman who is honest about who she is,
> with all her foibles and yet understanding that
> these are the backbone of who she has chosen to
> become, not because of them but despite them

I am a Woman who is resilient; knowing she's weathered many storms and can still find the belief that all is as it should be and that the sun will still warm her face on another dawning day
I am a Woman who is fearless in the face of what she believes she deserves, knowing she's fought for the right to be heard and to ask for her due
I am a Woman who is worthy of her aspirations, desires and dreams for she's earned the right through painstaking self examination
These are the intangible but most important for they show me how to be me.

A glorious opportunity awaits you to begin thinking + behaving + producing like the person you've always wanted to be now and for always. I wish you all the best as you walk your path.

> *May there always be work for your hands to do,*
> *May your purse always hold a coin or two.*
> *May the sun always shine warm on your windowpane,*
> *May a rainbow be certain to follow each rain.*
> *May the hand of a friend always be near you,*
> *And may God fill your heart with gladness to cheer you.*
> **~Irish proverb in honor of my Irish husband**

"A vida e o amor que criamos são a vida e o amor que vivemos." Translated: "The life and love we create is the life and love we live." ~Portuguese proverb in honor of my family.

CPSIA information can be obtained at www.ICGtesting.com
Printed in the USA
LVOW11s0232041016

507308LV00001B/16/P